APPLICATIONS OF PSY

Longman Essential Psychology
Series editor: Andrew M. Colman

Other titles in this series:

APPLICATIONS OF PSYCHOLOGY

EDITED BY

Andrew M. Colman

LONGMAN
London and New York

Addison Wesley Longman Limited
Edinburgh Gate
Harlow
Essex CM20 2JE, England
and Associated Companies throughout the world.

*Published in the United States of America
by Longman Publishing, New York*

© 1994 Routledge
This edition © 1995 Longman Group Limited
Compilation © 1995 Andrew Colman

This edition first published 1995
Second impression 1996

ISBN 0 582 27802 3 PPR

British Library Cataloguing-in-Publication Data
A catalogue record for this book is available from the British Library.

Library of Congress Cataloging-in-Publication Data
A catalogue record for this book is available from the Library of Congress.

Typeset by 25 in 10/12pt Times
Produced through Longman Malaysia, PP

CONTENTS

v

NOTES ON EDITORS AND CONTRIBUTORS

ANDREW M. COLMAN is Reader in Psychology at the University of Leicester, having previously taught at Rhodes and Cape Town Universities in South Africa. He is the founder and former editor of the journal *Current Psychology* and Chief Examiner for the British Psychological Society's Qualifying Examination. His books include *Facts, Fallacies and Frauds in Psychology* (1987), *What is Psychology? The Inside Story* (2nd edn, 1988), and *Game Theory and its Applications in the Social and Biological Sciences* (2nd edn, 1995).

PETER FONAGY took his doctorate in psychology at University College London and has been on the staff of its Department of Psychology since 1976. He is currently Freud Memorial Professor of Psychoanalysis at University College London. He is a clinical psychologist and psychoanalyst and member of the British Psycho-Analytical Society. He is coordinator of research at the Anna Freud Centre (Hampstead Child Therapy Clinic) and is a member of the Executive Council of the International Psychoanalytic Association. He has published articles in both psychoanalytic and psychological journals on numerous clinical and theoretical topics. He is co-author (with A. Higgitt) of *Personality Theory and Clinical Practice* (1984) and co-editor (with J. Sandler and E. S. Pearson) of *Freud's "On Narcissism": An Introduction* (1991).

DAVID FONTANA is Reader in Educational Psychology in the School of Education, University of Wales at Cardiff, and Professor Catedratico in the Department of Child Education, University of Minho, Portugal. A Fellow of the British Psychological Society and a Chartered Psychologist, he is the author of over 100 scientific papers and articles, and serves on the editorial boards of a number of psychological journals. He has written 15 books, including *The Education of the Young Child* (1984), *Behaviourism and Learning Theory in Education* (1984), *Classroom Control* (1985), *Teaching and Personality* (1986), *Psychology for Teachers* (1988), *Managing Stress*

(1989), and *Your Growing Child: From Birth to Adolescence* (1990). His books have been translated over 30 times into all major European languages.

CLIVE R. HOLLIN took his doctorate in psychology at the University of East London in 1980, after which he worked as a prison psychologist, then as a university lecturer. He currently holds the joint post of Senior Lecturer in Psychology at the University of Birmingham and Research Psychologist in the Youth Treatment Service. He is a fellow of the British Psychological Society and a Chartered Psychologist. He is co-editor of the journal *Psychology, Crime, and Law*. The author or editor of 11 books, including *Psychology and Crime* (1989), he has published numerous research articles, particularly on delinquency. His next book will be an ambitious attempt to blend core concepts from psychology and criminology in the search for a grand theory of criminal behaviour.

WENDY HOLLWAY taught in the Department of Occupational Psychology, Birkbeck College, University of London, for nine years and is now a Senior Lecturer at the University of Bradford. She is an associate fellow of the British Psychological Society and a Chartered Psychologist. She has published articles on the history of work psychology as it relates to current practices, books and articles on psychological theory and method concerning the understanding of subjectivity and gender, and articles concerning gender relations and discrimination in organizations. She is the author of *Work Psychology and Organisational Behaviour: Managing the Individual at Work* (1991).

GRAHAM E. POWELL is Director of Clinical Psychology Training at the University of Surrey. He qualified as a clinical psychologist at the Institute of Psychiatry, Maudsley Hospital, London, and is Director of Counselling Services to a British Police Force. He co-edited (with S. J. E. Lindsay) the first British textbook on clinical psychology, *A Handbook of Clinical Adult Psychology* (2nd edn, 1993). He is currently working on an analysis of the psychological factors underlying rate of progress in neurological rehabilitation.

SERIES EDITOR'S PREFACE

The *Longman Essential Psychology* series comprises twelve concise and inexpensive paperback volumes covering all of the major topics studied in undergraduate psychology degree courses. The series is intended chiefly for students of psychology and other subjects with psychology components, including medicine, nursing, sociology, social work, and education. Each volume contains five or six accessibly written chapters by acknowledged authorities in their fields, and each chapter includes a list of references and a small number of recommendations for further reading.

Most of the material was prepared originally for the Routledge *Companion Encyclopedia of Psychology* but with a view to later paperback subdivision – the contributors were asked to keep future textbook readers at the front of their minds. Additional material has been added for the paperback series: new co-editors have been recruited for nine of the volumes that deal with highly specialized topics, and each volume has a new introduction, a glossary of technical terms including a number of entries written specially for this edition, and a comprehensive new index.

I am grateful to my literary agents Sheila Watson and Amanda Little for clearing a path through difficult terrain towards the publication of this series, to Sarah Caro of Longman for her patient and efficient preparation of the series, to Brian Parkinson, David Stretch, and Susan Dye for useful advice and comments, and to Carolyn Preston for helping with the compilation of the glossaries.

ANDREW M. COLMAN

INTRODUCTION

Andrew M. Colman
University of Leicester, England

This volume surveys psychology's major practices and professions, which coexist alongside the academic discipline of psychology. The first four chapters cover the major professions of psychology, and chapter 5 deals with a practice that is closely associated with psychology but is not one of its own recognized professions.

Psychology emerged as an independent academic discipline in the 1880s, and for several decades thereafter psychologists confined their activities almost exclusively to teaching and research in universities and colleges. Starting in the 1950s, several new fields of applied psychology began to emerge, and eventually a range of non-academic professions of psychology developed. Psychologists began to find employment not only in universities and colleges, but also in hospitals, clinics, counselling agencies, specialized research establishments, schools, prisons, government departments, and commercial and industrial companies. In addition, many people built careers for themselves as self-employed professional psychologists in private practice. The major professions of psychology, discussed in detail in the chapters that follow, are clinical and counselling psychology (chapter 1); educational psychology, which is sometimes (especially in the United States) called school psychology (chapter 2); industrial (or occupational) and organizational psychology (chapter 3), and forensic (or criminological) psychology (chapter 4). In addition, there are a small number of practices that are closely allied to psychology but are not strictly part of it. Chapter 5 deals with an important example of this, namely psychoanalysis, which is a near relative of clinical and counselling psychology.

All of these practices and professions involve applying psychology to problems of everyday life. This contrasts sharply with basic research in academic psychology, in which understanding and explanation of behaviour and mental experience are regarded as sufficient ends in themselves, although practical applications are sometimes also of interest to basic researchers. Pure research can be considered important, irrespective of its immediate or potential usefulness for solving practical problems of everyday life, if it uncovers or helps to explain some previously unrecognized or poorly understood function or phenomenon of behaviour or mental experience. The professions of psychology, on the other hand, pursue essentially practical aims, although they rely on and exploit the findings of both pure and applied research. Clinical psychology, in helping people with all forms of mental disorder, relies on research into the nature, diagnosis, classification, treatment, and prevention of mental disorders. In educational (school) psychology, research into problems of learning, adjustment, and child behaviour is applied with the ultimate goal of offering practical help to troubled children, parents, and teachers. In industrial (occupational) and organizational psychology, research into the well-being and efficiency of people at work and in organizations is applied to the special problems that arise in those settings. Psychoanalysis is a slightly different case: it is an enormously influential theory of mental structure and function, based on the writings of Sigmund Freud (1856–1939) and his followers, and a highly specialized method of psychotherapy. The aims of psychoanalysis as a therapeutic method are similar to those of clinical and counselling psychology.

Outside the major professions discussed in this book, psychology finds subsidiary though none the less important applications in a variety of other fields. Some service industries, including market research, advertising, and management consultancy, often employ psychologists and make use of their special skills and knowledge. In addition, there are several professions, including nursing, social work, speech therapy, schoolteaching, and certain branches of medicine such as psychiatry and general practice, in which aspects of psychology are included in the basic training, and in which knowledge gained from psychological research is routinely applied in practice.

In some countries, there are legal barriers designed to prevent or limit the practice of psychology and pseudo-psychology by unqualified people. In the United States, some state legislatures have introduced certification laws that forbid practitioners who are not properly qualified from calling themselves psychologists, and others have introduced licensing laws that make it illegal for unqualified people to offer certain defined psychological services for payment. Licensing laws are uncommon in other parts of the world, but in Britain a voluntary Register of Chartered Psychologists was introduced in 1988. Only those on the Register of Chartered Psychologists are legally entitled to call themselves chartered psychologists and to receive practising certificates from the British Psychological Society. Most European countries, and many non-European countries including Australia, New Zealand, South Africa, and Japan, have some form of legal registration governing the practice of psychology.

In chapter 1 of this book, Graham E. Powell provides a survey of the approaches and techniques of clinical and counselling psychology, outlines the range of problems dealt with within these professions, and discusses certain associated professional issues. Powell points out that counselling psychology overlaps with clinical psychology to such a degree that it is difficult to separate them. Counselling is a broad and ill-defined term referring to a form of helping process that involves offering advice and information designed to assist individuals or groups of people in coping with their problems. It overlaps not only with clinical psychology, but also with educational or school psychology (chapter 2) and with aspects of industrial or occupational psychology (chapter 3) and forensic or criminological psychology (chapter 4). It includes the more specialized fields of marriage counselling, student counselling, vocational counselling, HIV and AIDS counselling, and rehabilitation counselling, although not all counsellors in these areas are psychologists.

Readers who wish to study the entire range of mental disorders that fall within clinical psychology should examine the *Diagnostic and Statistical Manual of Mental Disorders* published by the American Psychiatric Association, which provides an exhaustive classification of mental disorders and criteria for their diagnosis. The current edition (American Psychiatric Association, 1994) is generally referred to as *DSM–IV*, and its diagnostic criteria are widely accepted by clinical psychologists and other mental health practitioners worldwide. *DSM–IV* classifies mental disorders into the following categories: disorders usually first diagnosed in infancy, childhood, or adolescence; delirium, dementia, and amnestic and other cognitive disorders; mental disorders due to a general medical condition; substance-related disorders; schizophrenia and other pychotic disorders; mood disorders; anxiety disorders; somatoform disorders; factitious disorders; dissociative disorders; sexual and gender identity disorders; eating disorders; sleep disorders; impulse-control disorders not elsewhere classified; adjustment disorders; personality disorders; other conditions that may be a focus of clinical attention. Many abnormal psychology texts cover the entire range of *DSM–IV* categories, but in addition to the suggestions for further reading listed at the end of chapter 1, the book by Davison and Neale (1994) is highly recommended; and for more information on contemporary methods of treating the major disorders, see Barlow (1993).

Chapter 2, by David Fontana, focuses on educational or school psychology. Fontana starts by pointing out that the term *educational psychology* has a dual meaning, referring both to the psychology of education as it is taught to trainee schoolteachers and to the branch of applied professional psychology sometimes called school psychology devoted to helping children with learning and behavioural problems. One of the main functions of educational or school psychology in the latter sense is psychological assessment and diagnosis. For example, if a child is performing poorly at school, the child's parents or teachers may ask an educational psychologist to try to determine whether the problem is due to lack of ability, emotional disturbance, social or interpersonal problems with teachers or other children, difficulties in the home environment, some form of mental disorder, or (as is often the case) simply poor eyesight or hearing. Having diagnosed the problem, the educational or school psychologist may offer counselling or treatment in the form of individual, group, or family therapy, or may advise parents or teachers on therapeutic programmes that can be implemented in the home or at school. Therapeutic work with children has much in common with the techniques of clinical psychology but requires specialized skills for dealing with children and expertise in handling problems of educational adjustment. If the child is judged to have special educational needs, the educational psychologist may recommend specialized support services ranging up to placement in a special school or unit. Readers who wish to know more about educational or school psychology should consult the recommendations for further reading at the end of chapter 2 and perhaps also the book by Borich and Tombari (1995) or, for a more advanced discussion, the one by Pressley and McCormick (1995).

In chapter 3, Wendy Hollway discusses industrial (occupational) and organizational psychology. This branch of applied psychology is concerned with all aspects of psychology in the workplace and is commonly referred to in the United States as industrial/organizational psychology or simply I/O psychology and in Britain as occupational psychology. To avoid confusion Hollway prefers to use the simpler continental European term *work psychology*. Work psychology includes vocational guidance and selection, methods of dealing with problems of work motivation, job satisfaction and absenteeism in organizations, improvement of communication within organizations, design and implementation of training courses, teaching of social and human relations skills, improvement of promotion structures, evaluation of job performance, and counselling of employees about career development or retraining following redundancy or retirement.

Another source of terminological confusion surrounds an important branch of work psychology that is called ergonomics in Britain and the rest of Europe and engineering psychology in the United States. This is the application of psychology concerned with fitting jobs to people, rather than fitting people to jobs – fitting people to jobs falls under job selection and placement. Ergonomists design jobs, equipment, and workplaces to maximize performance and well-being and to minimize accidents, fatigue, boredom, and energy expenditure. Work psychology covers a vast and diverse range of activities, and readers wishing to read more about it should consult the suggestions for further reading at the end of chapter 3 and perhaps also the books by Smither (1994) and Steers and Black (1994).

In chapter 4, Clive R. Hollin provides a survey of forensic (criminological) psychology, a field of applied psychology that has been growing rapidly since the early 1980s. Within this broad field, research has flourished in many areas, from offender profiling to the design and evaluation of crime prevention programmes. Hollin confines his discussion to three of the most important groups of applications: psychology in the courtroom (including eyewitness testimony, confession evidence, and factors affecting jury decisions); theories of criminal behaviour, and crime prevention strategies. Chapter 4 does not discuss in detail certain other areas of forensic or criminological psychology that are closely related to clinical and counselling psychology. For example, psychologists employed in prisons and other penal institutions are often involved in the diagnostic assessment of inmates suffering from psychological disturbances such as depression, sleeplessness, uncontrollable anger, loss of identity, lack of assertiveness, guilt feelings, paranoia, and other psychological disturbances and forensic psychologists sometimes carry out individual and group therapy with psychologically disturbed inmates. For more information on this branch of applied psychology, see the further reading recommended, at the end of chapter 4 and the *Handbook of Psychology in Legal Contexts* (1995).

Chapter 5 is devoted to psychoanalysis. In this chapter Peter Fonagy, who is qualified as both a psychoanalyst and a clinical psychologist, distinguishes between psychoanalysis as a psychotherapeutic method of treatment, as a theory of mental disorder (especially of neurosis), as a theory of personality and individual differences, as a collection of theories about mental functioning, and even as a theory of human civilization. As a theory, psychoanalysis focuses primarily on unconscious mental processes and the various defence mechanisms that people use to repress them. As a therapeutic method, it involves 50-minute therapeutic sessions three or more times per week for several years, during which the psychoanalyst uses a number of specialized techniques to help the client uncover repressed thoughts and feelings, understand why they were repressed, and consciously accept them. Fonagy discusses the development of psychoanalytic theory from Freud's earliest ideas to the most important contributions of his followers, including Hartmann, Erikson, George Klein, Melanie Klein, Kernberg, Fairburn, Winnocott, and Kohut. The chapter includes a discussion of two forms of psychoanalysis as a treatment method – strict psychoanalysis and the more widely practised psychoanalytic psychotherapy that has evolved from it – and concludes with a general evaluation. For readers who wish to delve deeper into this subject, an alphabetically arranged reference work that is especially informative about the fundamental concepts of psychoanalysis is Laplanche and Pontalis's (1988) *The Language of Psycho-analysis*.

REFERENCES

American Psychiatric Association. (1994). *Diagnostic and statistical manual of mental disorders* (4th edn). Washington, DC: Author.

Barlow, D. H. (ed.). (1993). *Clinical handbook of psychological disorders: A step-by-step treatment manual*. New York: Guilford.

Borich, G. D., & Tombari, M. L. (1995). *Educational psychology: A contemporary approach*. New York: HarperCollins.

Davison, G. C., & Neale, J. M. (1994). *Abnormal psychology*. (6th edn). New York: Wiley.

Handbook of psychology in legal contexts. (1995). New York: Wiley.

Laplanche, J., & Pontalis, J.-B. (1988). *The language of psycho-analysis* translated by Nicholson-Smith, London: Karnac Books and The Institute of Psycho-analysis. (Original work published 1967.)

Pressley, M., & McCormick, C. B. (1995). *Advanced educational psychology for educators, researchers and policy makers*. New York: HarperCollins.

Smither R. D. (1994). *The psychology of work and human performance* (2nd edn). London: HarperCollins.

Steers, R. M., & Black, J. S. (1994). *Organizational behavior* (5th edn). London: HarperCollins.

1

CLINICAL AND COUNSELLING PSYCHOLOGY

Graham E. Powell

University of Surrey, England

Models and approaches
 Behaviourism and behaviour
  therapy
 Cognitive behaviour
  modification
  cognitive therapy
 Rational-emotive therapy
 Social learning theory
 Attributional approaches
 Personal construct theory
 Person- or client-centred
  therapy
 Gestalt therapy
 Existential therapy
 Systems approaches
 Freudian theory
 Post-Freudian developments
 Eclecticism
 Evaluation of models

Problems and their management
 The definition of a problem
 Stress
 Anxiety and panic
 Phobias
 Obsessions and compulsions
 Depression
 Interpersonal problems
 Marital and relationship
  problems
 Health problems
 Contribution to different
  client groups
Professional issues
 Range of roles
 Training
 Code of conduct
Further reading
References

Clinical and counselling psychology are the two professional branches of the discipline of psychology which together form a seamless robe comprising the application of psychological knowledge to the maintenance of mental and physical health and the generation of psychological well-being. They overlap

1

to the extent that they both draw on the same sources, namely the empirical knowledge generated by scientific studies and research, and the theoretical knowledge as embodied in a wide range of principles, models, and approaches. They both espouse the scientist-practitioner model of helping people. This means that clinical and counselling psychologists are trained in both scientific method (for example, statistics, research design, evaluation) and in practical skills (for example, treatment and assessment methods and professional skills). It also implies that a broadly scientific approach is taken with clients: making objective observations, collecting the required information, formulating a psychological explanation for the problems at hand, developing an approach to dealing with the problem, and monitoring progress carefully, revising ideas as necessary in the light of progress and new developments (Brammer, Shostrom, & Abrego, 1989). However, the emphases of clinical and counselling psychology are different. Clinical psychology has a longer professional history, and has its roots in the development of psychometric assessment methods and the management of mental illness, while counselling psychology has developed out of the need for people to make decisions about their problems and to make psychological growth in terms of their abilities to help themselves. I shall make no further attempt to distinguish the two, and will concentrate on how psychology as a whole is used to help people with behavioural, cognitive or emotional difficulties.

The plan of this chapter is to divide the field, first, by the models and approaches that are used to guide the helping process – such theories provide a framework for observation, formulation, and treatment, and can be developed to advance fundamental knowledge – and second, by the commonest problems presented by clients. Finally, I shall mention training and professional issues.

MODELS AND APPROACHES

Behaviourism and behaviour therapy

The roots of behaviourism are in operant conditioning, in which behaviour is shaped by the positive and negative rewards or reinforcements that follow it, and classical conditioning, in which psychophysiological responses such as anxiety become associated with stimuli in the environment that happen to be around when this response is experienced (see Bandura, 1969). Treatment begins with an analysis of what stimuli trigger the behaviour that is the problem, and what consequences follow from emitting this behaviour. The treatments themselves often stem directly from the work of Skinner (1974) on how rats learn to press a lever for food, and Pavlov's (1927) on how dogs can come to salivate to the sound of a bell. If the client wishes to strengthen a behaviour, then positive reinforcement can be arranged for it. If new behaviours are to be learned, they can be "shaped up" by expecting and

2

rewarding closer and closer approximations and by arranging for the right environmental cues or triggers to be present. New behaviour can also be learned by having it modelled by others, and all new behaviours can be maintained by ensuring that some intermittent reinforcement continues. Inappropriate behaviour can be eliminated by having the person keep doing it until sated, by removing any positive reinforcement, or by arranging for an incompatible behaviour to be elicited by the triggering stimuli. Emotional "behaviour" can be modified by deconditioning, breaking the association that has been built up between, say, anxiety and the presence of thunder. This is known as desensitization. Conversely, a negative emotion, such as disgust, can be deliberately conditioned to something that is liked too much, perhaps alcohol. This is known as sensitization.

Behaviour therapy rapidly won many advocates because of its clarity of model and scientific approach, and throughout the 1960s empirical studies emerged on treating phobias, inability to relax, inappropriate sexual attractions, sexual problems, obsessions, enuresis, disruptive behaviour, deficits in self-help skills, problems in rehabilitation, and so forth. However, this impressive contribution to the skills of the clinician or counsellor could not disguise its limitations. It tended to be mechanistically applied; there were still many treatment failures, often to do with cognitive aspects such as motivation; it had little success with several important and common problems, especially depression; and models of learning taking over from those of Skinner and Pavlov were explicitly beginning to recognize cognitive factors. For example, the clients' expectations or beliefs about reward contingencies are often just as important as the actual contingencies themselves. Behaviourism, then, has been a tremendous spur but is somewhat limited in application and is not a comprehensive theory of human behaviour. Later cognitive and cognitive-behavioural approaches developed, and some of them will be discussed next.

Cognitive behaviour modification

Meichenbaum (1977) developed and investigated the theme that how you talk to yourself is crucial in determining both behaviour and feelings. Since self-guiding speech directs much of what we do, it becomes an appropriate target for assessment and treatment. The general strategy is to identify dysfunctional self-speech, for example, "I knew I would never do it right anyway", and to teach adaptive strategies, for example, "It's not going well, but I can see what the problem is and I must work out a plan to solve it". Initially, the client practises self-speech aloud and then silently until it is habitual. Self-praising statements are also practised. Applications have included anger control, stress management, coping with anxiety, and social skills.

3

Cognitive therapy

Beck and his colleagues (Beck, Rush, Shaw, & Emery, 1977) have extensively studied the influence on behaviour and emotions of what people think and say about themselves and the world. They have found that problems are frequently associated with warped or erroneous thinking. Such thoughts must be identified and reformulated, and this changes the way that stimuli in the environment are perceived, interpreted, and ultimately reacted to. In other words, this approach concerns the cognitive interface between stimulus and response that was not acknowledged in classic behaviourism. In treatment, the client learns that the perception of reality is different from reality and that such perceptions are often based on faulty thinking. The client tries to observe his or her own thoughts objectively and identifies distortions in thinking, such as over-reactions, over-generalizations, and a failure to take into account all the relevant information. The client then practises arguing against and countering these distortions, putting it in writing first and practising until it becomes habitual. The technique shows particular promise in relation to depression and anxiety disorder, and is generating a good deal of empirical research.

Rational-emotive therapy

Ellis (Ellis & Whitely, 1979) introduced logic and reason into counselling in quite an extreme way. He pointed out that people hold beliefs that cause problems and that thinking about problems is often muddled. He set out to make people appreciate what assumptions or rules about life they were making and to rationally consider whether other assumptions or rules were more logical and helpful in terms of adjustment. Common irrational ideas or values are that it is essential to be loved by everyone; that a person must be perfectly competent; that it is easier to avoid difficulties than to face them; and that the influence of past events are the determinants of present behaviour and cannot be eradicated. Rational-emotive therapy (RET) is a process of detection and reeducation, with dispute and discussion of how such beliefs are contributing to a problem and whether such beliefs should not be rethought and changed. As with cognitive therapy, with which RET plainly overlaps, this method has been particularly examined in relation to depression and anxiety, but it is also relevant to many quality-of-life issues, such as adjusting to role change during the lifespan and recurrent difficulties in personal relationships.

Social learning theory

Bandura (1986) developed a model of behaviour centred on the finding that people can learn many complex skills through observation alone, that is, by a process of modelling, rather than by overt practice. He therefore stressed the cognitive mediation of learning in which people do not learn by piecemeal trial and error, but acquire whole patterns which, when emitted in their entirety, may then be subject to reinforcement – for example the abused child who may then abuse as an adult. Learning is taken to be specific to situations, and so the role of traits in determining behaviour is seen to be much less than normally believed. However, people can *believe* in cross-situational consistency and this can cause problems. This is especially important in relation to "self-efficacy", which is perceived competence to be able to do something. Clients often over-generalize, and if their confidence or competence in just one area is challenged or undermined, they often feel incompetent across the board and self-evaluations become negative. In therapy, the perception of self-efficacy is defined and discussed and the client tries to develop skills, normally by a series of practice steps, in those areas where self-efficacy is judged lowest. These ideas have for the most part been incorporated into related therapies rather than standing alone as a therapy, and have helped develop the experimental literature.

Attributional approaches

Attribution theory (Jones et al., 1972) stems from the research literature on how people explain their own and others' behaviour. Attributions of the same event may differ between people. If two people receive an invitation to a party, one may see it as a reflection of friendship, and the other may feel invited out of duty or politeness. Some people may believe that they failed an exam because it was very hard, others because they are useless. Misattributions can cause problems and misunderstandings, especially if they cause people to deny their own abilities and qualities, and this is especially true in the case of depression and social anxiety. Therapy consists of identifying the clients' explanations and changing dysfunctional ones, by a consideration of alternative explanations. These ideas have been incorporated into several related therapies, particularly cognitive therapy and rational-emotive therapy.

Personal construct theory

Kelly (1955) developed a highly articulated and coherent theory of personality, called personal construct theory (PCT), which has generated a large and growing body of empirical literature. The central notion is that people make sense of the world by judging or "construing" events on a set of internal, bipolar, cognitive "constructs" or dimensions, such as *this will be stressful for me* versus *I will be able to relax*, or *upsetting* versus *irrelevant to me emotionally*. This helps people anticipate subsequent events and to adjust their behaviour accordingly, or to react accordingly. Every individual has a different set of constructs because each has had different experiences. Individuals will also vary in the number of constructs they have, how they are organised, the degree to which they are shared with other people, and the ease with which they can be modified. Problems in life often stem from a mis-construing of events, so events might seem threatening when they should not be, and there may be distressing misunderstandings of other people, especially partners. Problems also arise when new events come along that cannot easily be construed or when our most basic constructs are called into question. Therapy consists of changing troublesome construct systems. The constructs are elicited and the construing of key events defined. The construct system is thus opened up to discussion and also to validation by careful observation of events from then on. PCT has a wide range of application including couple counselling, specific anxieties, social skills problems, coping with stammering and other stigma, and preparing for role transitions.

Having dealt with the main cognitive-behavioural approaches, we shall turn to three "humanist" approaches which aim primarily to help people get in touch with themselves and to acknowledge their true feelings. We shall then tackle systems approaches, followed by Freudian and related models.

Person- or client-centred therapy

Rogers (1942) began an influential movement in which the self-generated and self-propelled growth of the individual is given paramount importance and respect. The therapist does not judge or condemn the clients' beliefs or plans, does not give specific advice or instruction, and does not give advice on how in general to live. The client, not the therapist, develops the treatment plan, the direction of the dialogue comes from the client, and it is not the therapist who interprets the client's experience. The therapist tries to create an atmosphere of non-possessive warmth, accurate empathy, and genuineness, and these three aspects of the relationship have generated a variety of empirical research into the psychotherapeutic process (Truax & Carkhuff, 1967). Warmth involves acceptance and respect and caring to help build client trust, motivation, and willingness to communicate. Empathy exists when therapists can decentre or see things from the client's perspective, setting aside their own feelings and understanding what the client would be experiencing. These feelings are reflected back to the client who comes to feel understood and to develop self-understanding. Genuineness implies honesty, openness, and a degree of self-disclosure, which can give feedback to clients on what effect their behaviour is having on another person, the therapist. By the end of the therapy, it is hoped that the client will be more open to their experiences and less defensive, be more realistic in perceiving events and in self-perception, have a more positive self-regard, and be more effective at independent problem solving.

Gestalt therapy

Perls (1973) encapsulated a tradition of analysis of the here-and-now and the sharing of that experience in a therapeutic relationship. The goal is to promote growth by increasing awareness and insight, and in this there are obvious similarities to client-centred therapy. Gestalt therapy involves exploration with the therapist providing direct experience. Three principles of therapy have been described. "I and thou" implies an open, shared therapeutic climate, "what and how" refers to exercises to expand the clients' experiences, and "here and now" reinforces the orientation of the therapy to present, actual experience. Gestalt approaches have not been subject to any great amount of empirical research, which is in part a consequence of the ethos of the movement and the lack of precision in specifying models and methods. But some of the techniques are appealing, for example the empty chair technique in which the client switches between two chairs as he or she role-plays both sides of an argument, and the notion of unfinished business (that is, an incomplete Gestalt) is in common parlance.

Existential therapy

This is rooted in the philosophy of existentialism, and is an approach more than a specific therapy, although it is often described as such. The notion of phenomenology, from which existentialism developed, is that all knowledge is subjective and that the client has to clear the path of accurate perception by examining preconceptions and assumptions, to consider things in fresh ways. The work of Laing (1974) in attempting to understand schizophrenia is an example of how the existential perspective can lead to a new way of looking at old problems. However, it is a diffuse and fragmented movement which has not resulted as yet in much empirical research, or even systematic description and discussion of methods.

Systems approaches

There is no one model here but a widely endorsed movement which emphasizes the context of the behaviour as an explanation or cause, whereas many other approaches emphasize individuals themselves as responsible for their own behaviour. The relationship system of the client (for example, family, friends, working colleagues) is examined and the meaning or importance of the problem behaviour for the relevant system drawn out. For example, a child's school refusal may be instrumental in preventing the parents from splitting up. There is an inter-generational approach which suggests that the origin of difficulties lies with the previous generation and that trends are passed on and elaborated until emerging as a real problem. Structural therapies focus on family problems and try to help a family develop an internal structure or organization, involving boundary definition, that allows for both a sense of belonging and individuation. Strategic therapy focuses on the problem as the unit to be treated and how a system comes to be organized about a problem, often reinforcing it in the process. Much of the empirical work in this field has been with the families of children presenting problems, and a range of studies show how useful this approach can be (Minuchin & Fishman, 1981).

Freudian theory

Freud (1943) developed a model of personality which dramatically changed the way that a whole society thought about people, their behaviour, and their problems.

Freud described how the mind or psyche is divided metaphorically into the id (unconscious energy for the mind comprising all the basic drives such as urges for affection, warmth, food and sex, present from birth), the ego (developing later in the first year of life and dealing with reality), and the superego (the personality including morals, standards, and conscience). The interplay between these three is referred to as psychodynamics. For example, the id operates on a pleasure principle, wanting immediate gratification of any unmet need, but the ego realises that this is not the most effective way of dealing with reality and planning life. In developing a personality structure, a person goes through various stages to do with what gratifies the id. These are the oral stage (sucking and feeding), anal stage (elimination and retention), phallic stage (around age 5–6 years, involving stimulation of the genitalia), latency period (reduced interest in sex until about 12 years old), and genital stage (adult heterosexual interest).

Problems can arise in a variety of ways. For example, development can become "stuck" or fixated at a certain stage if the appropriate balance is not achieved between what the id wants and what the environment can provide. Another example of problems occurring is neurotic anxiety, which stems from the blockage of unconscious impulses. The ego can defend against feeling this anxiety by various mechanisms such as repression (pushing impulses into the unconscious), projection (perceiving the emotion as existing in other people rather than oneself), displacement (redirecting the emotion into something acceptable), and rationalization (inventing an acceptable reason for the emotion).

The classic therapy, psychoanalysis, is concerned with how the ego reacts with anxiety when a repressed impulse pushes for expression. It can be seen that such anxiety can be the effect of conflicts from a long time previously that were repressed rather than solved. The patient may be asked to free associate, and the chain of such associations or blocks to saying certain things gives clues to sensitivities and repressed areas. Dreams may be analysed, because during sleep the defence of the ego is relaxed and repressed material may emerge. The therapist will offer interpretations of associations, dreams, behaviour, and resistance to therapy, in the hope of lifting repression and thereby stimulating insight, understanding, and adjustment. Healthy impulses are to be freed and the superego is to encourage humane and not punitive standards.

Particular interpretation is made of transference, which occurs when attitudes and feelings from an earlier life situation are apparent in the client's behaviour towards the therapist in either a positive or negative direction (for example, either friendliness, love, and affection, or hostility and anger). The client is helped to see that relationships, in this case with the therapist, are being influenced unduly by issues that are not now pertinent. (Sometimes there is counter-transference, when the therapist transfers elements from his or her past on to the analytic relationship with the client, and so therapists are trained to be aware of this and to avoid it.)

Freud's ideas and methods have drawn criticism from both within the movement (overemphasis on the id and lack of recognition of the role of the ego; relative balance of instincts versus sociocultural factors; and an overemphasis of sexuality) and from scientific psychologists (limited range of application of treatments; based on a small and biased sample of people; ill-defined and diffuse methods; outcomes that are very difficult to define or operationalize). But no one denies the brilliance of debate that Freud stimulated.

Post-Freudian developments

Jung (1982) in his "analytical psychology" de-emphasized the sexual nature of the libido and saw it as representing a more general biological force, and introduced the concept of the "collective unconscious" in addition to our own personal unconscious. This is the repository of people's experiences over the centuries.

Adler (1929) developed "individual psychology". In doing so he attributed less of a role to instincts and developed the importance and relevance of striving for superiority, dominance, and mastery, all in a manner that is compatible with the needs of society and the social good.

Erickson (1959) examined closely how the ego developed an identity through the process of psychosocial development. Instead of seeing development as virtually ending early in life, he espoused a "lifespan development psychology", in which people grow psychologically to the moment of death.

An important psychodynamic development since Freud has been object relations therapy. This concerns past interpersonal relationships and how childhood experience can unconsciously determine adult patterns of behaviour. Patterns of living and lifestyle are formed by early relationships and repeated in many variations through life. The task of the therapist is to uncover this process and thereby encourage change in the repeating pattern of living, hopefully to a less problematic one (Eagle, 1984; Klein, 1975).

Eclecticism

Eclecticism is not a theory but a way of working which involves drawing on aspects from different models. It is productive if it encourages awareness of a variety of processes, open-mindedness, a critical appreciation of what therapeutic tools are available, and a desire to fit the treatment to the client, rather than vice versa. It is poor practice if it stems from an unwillingness or inability to make discriminations between the quality, applicability, and efficacy of methods, or from a naïve belief that all approaches are equal, or if different approaches are used without a genuine attempt to integrate them.

Evaluation of models

All models and approaches should be examined and evaluated for strength and weakness in order for them to improve and grow. Good models will have clearly stated principles which can be identified sufficiently well to be challenged; basic concepts should be defined and unambiguous; the range of applicability will be made explicit; methods and techniques will be defined sufficiently well to be understood and acquired by others; a body of empirical research will build up to identify the model as valuable in terms of its ability to predict and explain human behaviour and cognition; a similar body of empirical research will be established as regards efficacy of outcome (Smith, Glass, & Miller 1980). Poor models will have diffuse and ambiguous principles difficult to pin down sufficiently well to challenge; will have difficulty in specifying the essential skills to be taught to potential therapists; methods and techniques will seem ad hoc; explanatory concepts will be unreasonable or weak; there may be internal inconsistencies in the model as a whole; and a body of empirical data will not have been stimulated, especially in relation to outcome or efficacy (Garfield & Bergin, 1986). There is widespread support for the effectiveness of the behaviour therapies and good support for the effectiveness, range of applicability, and general usefulness of some of the cognitive-behavioural methods, especially rational-emotive therapy. There is a burgeoning research interest in cognitive therapy, which has made a special name for itself in regard to depression, and deservedly so. In the systems area, the structural models have been particularly well supported. Psychodynamic (Freudian and post-Freudian) therapies for a long time were removed from traditional scientific evaluation, but this is now changing (Horowitz, 1988) and one senses that important areas of efficacy will emerge. Of the humanistic approaches, client-centred therapy stands out in terms of supporting research.

PROBLEMS AND THEIR MANAGEMENT

The definition of a problem

There is no straightforward dividing line between concepts such as "normal–abnormal", "functional–dysfunctional", or "problematic–problem free". For example, one definition of abnormal is statistical, when the behaviour or capacity in question is rare (for example, those with an uncommonly low IQ); another is to do with suffering, so that something is abnormal if it involves marked personal distress, such as in bereavement; another definition is to do with disability, such as the effect of substance abuse on work performance; a further definition concerns whether the behaviour violates a social norm, such as the sociopath's callousness towards others. In psychiatry, abnormalities and problems are defined in the American Psychiatric Association's *Diagnostic and Statistical Manual of Mental Disorders* (3rd edition, revised), often referred to simply as DSM-III-R (American Psychiatric Association, 1987). It is a useful summary of the most serious problems that people face. There are five dimensions or axes.

Axis I covers clinical syndromes: disruptive behaviour disorders; anxiety disorders of childhood or adolescence; eating disorders; gender identity disorders; tic disorders; elimination disorders; speech disorders not elsewhere classified; other disorders of infancy, childhood, or adolescence; dementia arising in the senium and presenium; psychoactive substance-induced organic mental disorders; organic mental disorders associated with physical disorders; psychoactive substance use disorders; schizophrenia; delusional (paranoid) disorder; psychotic disorders not elsewhere classified; mood disorders; anxiety disorders; somatoform disorders; dissociative disorders; sexual disorders; sleep disorders; factitious disorders; impulse control disorders not classified elsewhere; adjustment disorder; psychological factors affecting physical condition.

Axis II covers developmental and personality disorders: mental retardation; pervasive developmental disorder; specific developmental disorders; other developmental disorders; personality disorders (Cluster A, paranoid, schizoid, schizotypal; Cluster B, antisocial, borderline, histrionic, narcissistic; Cluster C, avoidant, dependent, obsessive compulsive, passive aggressive).

On Axis III are the physical conditions and disorders. Axis IV and V are for research purposes, and are a severity scale and global functioning scale respectively.

There are a number of substantial criticisms of DSM-III-R. For example, words such as "elevated" or "excessive" are not defined and are a judgement on the part of the therapist; there seems to be little empirical evidence for grouping certain symptoms together into a "syndrome"; and the reliability and validity of the categories is generally unknown or uncertain. From a psychological perspective, it has been argued that one should measure symptoms and then see which ones cluster together to form syndromes, and not start with the premise that particular syndromes exist. None the less, DSM-III-R has provided a much-needed common and for the most part neutral language with which to describe problems and to carry out preliminary differential diagnosis. It is then a matter for the psychologist to provide a psychological explanation for the specific problems of the specific patient.

Some of the common ways of treating particular types of problems will now be described.

Stress

When stressed, we prepare our bodies for fight or flight. Powerful stimulants such as adrenalin are released into the bloodstream, along with thyroid hormones to increase metabolism and cholesterol to boost energy. These chemicals, if released on a long-term basis, can cause heart disease and strokes, exhaustion, weight loss, and hardening of the arteries – good reasons to cope with stress effectively. Other reasons are to do with our performance, in that with chronic stress, concentration and attention decrease, memory and speed of thinking become patchy, error rates increase, long-term planning deteriorates, and thinking becomes more confused and irrational (Powell & Enright, 1990). In addition, physical tension increases, personality changes, people feel depressed and helpless, self-esteem falls, interests diminish, sleep is disrupted, drug abuse rises, and people stop trying to solve the fundamental problems. The most stressful sorts of experiences are such things as death of a spouse, divorce or separation, and personal injury or illness. Medium stresses are taking on a major mortgage, changing one's line of work, or having more arguments with one's spouse. Lower level stresses are caused by having a change in sleeping habits, social activities, or vacations. Personality is also important. Particularly vulnerable to self-induced stress are people with Type A behaviours – those who feel an intense sense of time urgency, inappropriate hostility, and aggression, always try to do two things at once, and who try to achieve goals without proper planning.

A variety of methods are helpful. Insight into the situation is mandatory; the individual must recognize the emotional and behavioural patterns as a reaction to stress, and the precise stresses have to be identified, not always an easy matter if the client is "denying" certain sources of stress. A plan has to be made about how to tackle each of the stresses, perhaps by using a client-centred approach to reinforce the clients themselves as the main agents of change. Solutions to some problems may need other kinds of help. For example, if one of the sources of stress is taking on too much work, the client may need assertion training to learn to say "no". If another source of stress is taking on a new financial responsibility, then a cognitive approach could be taken to turn dysfunctional thoughts ("I could be bankrupt tomorrow") into more realistic ones ("This new business loan has been very well planned and there are many things I can do to help the expansion succeed"). A self-instruction approach can be used to cope with the immediate unpleasant emotional feelings ("I have coped with this sort of problem before", "If I can look the problem in the eye it will help", "I know I am feeling on the edge, but I have made sensible plans to improve the situation"). Finally, the client may well have some difficult decision to make about setting clear life goals and priorities.

Anxiety and panic

There are two main kinds of anxiety state (Barlow, Blanchard, Vermilyea, Vermilyea, & Di Nardo, 1986). First, when the main problem is one of panic attacks, there is a sudden overwhelming feeling of apprehension and fear coupled with a wide variety of intense physical distress symptoms such as palpitations, trembling, and dizziness, which often make clients feel that they are dying or going mad. Second, when there is excessive anxiety and worry in general, a variety of chronic feelings such as fatiguability, insomnia, irritability, and restlessness develop. In anxiety the individual systematically overestimates the danger or difficulty of a situation, and there are many negative automatic thoughts and dysfunctional assumptions and rules. For example, with generalized anxiety, people who experience anxiety in social situations may say very little for fear of being ridiculed, but this makes them outsiders, reinforcing their belief that they are likely to be rejected. Dysfunctional rules, such as "Everything must be done perfectly or I will fail" or "Anyone who criticizes me dislikes me", are common. In panic disorders, the main dysfunctional element is the tendency to interpret bodily sensation in a catastrophic fashion. For example, feeling breathless after walking fast to make an appointment on time becomes a palpitation signalling an imminent heart attack, or a racing of thoughts becomes imminent total loss of mental control. The first step in treatment is to develop an objective insight into these processes, often by taking careful notes about what one is thinking or feeling when anxious or when about to panic, or by discussing a recent experience in detail.

The dysfunctional beliefs identified can then be challenged, by gauging the evidence for the thought, asking how another person would feel, asking whether all the facts have been taken into account, asking whether one is thinking in an all-or-none manner, gauging whether the degree of control is being underestimated, considering whether one is overestimating the negative consequences, or asking whether one is underestimating the skills and problem-solving abilities that can be brought to bear. Distraction techniques can also be used, for example concentrating on actual performance rather than the associated negative thoughts, and there can be behavioural experiments, such as hyperventilating to produce dizziness to prove this does not cause a heart attack. More behavioural methods can be used to reduce avoidant behaviour, gradually reintroducing clients into feared situations in a calm way to break up the association with anxiety. This technique is called desensitization.

Phobias

Desensitization is worth describing in some detail as it is one of the most widely applied and effective of behavioural methods (Du Pont, 1982). The main types of phobia are simple (for example, irrational fear of blood, heights), social (for example, irrational fear of negative evaluation, feelings of rejection), or agoraphobia (for example, irrational fear of being trapped or confined, being far from home). The symptoms include marked avoidance of the feared situations, anxiety, or even panic when actually in them, and dysfunctional beliefs about what there is to worry about. The aim in desensitization is to unlearn the association between the situation and anxiety, by a series of graded exposures, to bring the client nearer to the object of fear in a series of small and manageable steps. Each step is repeated until minimal anxiety is felt before moving on to the next step. At each step, once contact is made the person resolves not to withdraw until the anxiety lessens, because withdrawing from a situation while anxiety is at its highest would only make the phobia worse. If one is afraid of heights, the hierarchy could begin with standing on a staircase looking down, moving on to leaning out of a first-floor window, then climbing a ladder, walking across a bridge, then sitting at the top of a cliff face, and finally looking out from the top of a tower block. In fact, it is not always necessary to do these things in real life. Working up a graduated hierarchy in one's imagination, known as "imaginal desensitization", can also be very effective, and at least will reduce some of the anticipatory anxiety prior to doing things in real life – "*in vivo* desensitization". Supplementary techniques will concern managing anxiety until it reduces (for example, relaxation, distraction, and challenging dysfunctional thoughts), and having the therapist model appropriate coping.

Obsessions and compulsions

Obsessions are unwanted thoughts, images, and impulses which intrude into thinking and behaviour. The person usually sees them as senseless, useless, and often repugnant or very distressing, but they cannot be easily dismissed. The obsession may be triggered by a variety of things, such as the presence of dirt or a certain sort of item on the news, perhaps about a murder; this causes a variety of uncomfortable feelings which are neutralized by performing compulsive behaviour or thought (for example, washing, or thoroughly checking where one was at the time of the murder). These compulsions are frequently highly stereotyped, for example washing the hands in a particular

14

way with a certain depth of water at a certain temperature, taking the fingers one at a time in a strict order, then the palms, and finally the backs of the hands. These compulsions bring temporary relief from the anxiety (Turner & Beidel, 1988); anxiety is also reduced by the great deal of avoidance that is built up to prevent coming across the triggers in the first place. The two arms of treatment are therefore first, to expose the person gradually to those things that are being avoided, and second, to encourage ways of coping with the triggers that do not involve the compulsions, a technique often referred to as response prevention. The rationale for treatment is presented in the context of how the pattern of behaviour may have developed (perhaps, for example, the child had similar patterns modelled or encouraged by parents) and how the person reacts to the triggers (for example, dysfunctional thoughts) or what they believe to be the utility of the compulsions (irrational beliefs). Next, the patient is exposed to a gradual hierarchy of triggers. The therapist models appropriate coping, which is copied by the patient, who agrees to delay performing the compulsion until the anxiety has reduced. Feedback is given as to how the anxiety is reduced each time response prevention is practised, and how the thoughts about the triggers and compulsions change.

Depression

The word depression describes a mood (unhappy, fed-up, self-deprecating, listless, apathetic) and a syndrome (depressed mood, loss of interest, anxiety, sleep disturbance, loss of appetite and energy, suicidal thoughts). Depression can also be subdivided, for example into bipolar (swinging from low to high mood), endogenous (no obvious cause), and reactive (attributable to the effects of an identifiable experience). Sometimes these problems are treated by physical methods such as antidepressant medication including tricyclics and lithium, but increasingly the efficacy of psychological methods, especially cognitive therapy, are being acknowledged. Dobson (1989) found that cognitive therapy patients did better than 98 per cent of non-treatment controls, 67 per cent of behaviour therapy clients, 70 per cent of antidepressant clients, and 70 per cent of other psychotherapy clients. It will be recalled from earlier in this chapter that depressed affect is held in cognitive therapy to be the result of negative thoughts and negatively biased perceptions. There is a "negative triad" involving self (seen as inadequate and defective), life (seen as making extreme demands and repeatedly defeating the person), and the future (bound to hold failure). Early in treatment the problem is assessed, the patient is taught about the model, and any pessimism about treatment has to be tackled. Patients are taught how to list their thoughts on a record sheet, noting when they happened, the situation they were in, and the emotions that accompanied them. The intensity of the emotion and degree of belief in the thought can be rated on a scale. The automatic negative thoughts thus identified are then systematically challenged, just as described earlier in relation to anxiety. Once this can be done, more general maladaptive assumptions, such as Ellis's "irrational beliefs" can be similarly approached. Many problems can arise in cognitive therapy for depression including lack of collaboration, over-anticipation of failure, lack of the skills necessary to carry out homework assignments (for example, to tackle a financial problem or deal with a difficult work colleague in a different way), lack of motivation, trying to move too fast, and worries about the consequence of change. Each of these needs to be tackled within therapy, and other techniques or approaches can be used to circumvent the problem (for example, social skills training for the client who would not try behaving with his work colleagues in a different way). New applications of cognitive therapy concern group treatment approaches, therapy for those with long-term mild but chronic depression, identifying negative thought patterns established early in childhood, and specific groups such as adult survivors of child sex abuse.

Interpersonal problems

Quite a wide variety of effective methods for tackling the enhancement of interpersonal competence are now available (Spence, 1993). In overt behavioural social skills training, the micro-skills (for example, eye contact, posture) and macro-skills (for example, giving compliments, making a complaint, and so on), are both taught. Training begins with instruction, coaching, and discussion, and the therapist will model appropriate skills. The session will include behavioural rehearsal or role-playing, about which feedback and reinforcement are given. The client will then have homework assignments to do. Another treatment is training in social-perception skills, to help the person identify the appropriate dynamic cues in others. The client then imagines and carries out various possible responses to these cues and monitors his or her own dynamic cues and how they influence communication. There can also be training in social problem-solving skills when possible solutions to problems are critically examined to evaluate likely outcomes of each so that the most suitable course can be chosen. Of particular importance in forensic work is training in affect control, especially anger. The client is taught to identify the situations that trigger anger and are trained to "stop" rather than react when the trigger occurs, and to use interpersonal problem-solving strategies as just discussed. Finally, the role of maladaptive cognitions again has to be acknowledged and cognitive therapy methods are again relevant.

Marital and relationship problems

Much of the early empirical work on marital and relationship problems was quite behavioural in nature and centred on the notion that partners exchange or reciprocate behaviours or reinforcers (reciprocity). Marital disharmony arises when rates of exchange are low, problem-solving skills poor, rates of conflict produced by the behaviour high, and when the behaviours exchanged are mainly negative (negative reciprocity). Interactions therefore comprise communication training, training in problem-solving skills and the negotiation of a "contract" to exchange behaviours that are constructive and rewarding to the other person (Jacobson & Gurman, 1986). These methods have developed by application of a more cognitive approach. Perceptions of what events occur are compared; attributions about why these events happened are analysed; expectations about the future become important; and the couple's general assumptions or beliefs drawn out. For example, a thoughtlessly hurtful word by a partner can be perceived as a deliberate needle, attributed to a malign intent to cause distress, confirming the expectation that the relationship will be hurtful in the future, and be worsened by an underlying belief that once a relationship goes wrong it cannot be retrieved. Systems theory approaches are also very important. The therapist works with the clients to produce a map of the organisation, roles, boundaries, and rules of the relationship. The concepts of enmeshment and disengagement are especially relevant. An enmeshed style is when there is little separateness or autonomy — the couple will think or act as one. At the opposite end of the spectrum, in a disengaged style, the couple make minimal contact and provide little support in difficult times. Treatment aims to help couples adopt an appropriate style in relation to any particular life task. For example, one needs to be enmeshed to deal with crises, but more disengaged when one partner is striving to confirm his or her identity.

Health problems

Increasingly, psychologists are contributing to the maintenance of physical health. Two examples illustrate this in regard to asthma and diabetes. Asthma is an intermittent difficulty in breathing due to bronchoconstriction, and swelling and mucus secretion in the lungs. It can be precipitated by irritants such as pollen or smoke, physical agitation, and the intake of cold air. A psychological package to help children cope has been developed by Creer (1982). Children as young as 5 years of age can be taught to identify the first stage of an attack and then to adopt a coping routine involving a restriction of physical activity, relaxation to counter any feelings of panic, and drinking a warm liquid. Once settled, the bronchodilator may be used.

Diabetes occurs when the pancreas fails to produce enough insulin to metabolise glucose, leading to heart disease and circulatory problems. Changes in blood glucose are notably related to psychological stress. The role of psychological intervention concerns the situation in which the diabetes is poorly controlled, particularly in children. The child is taught how to monitor his or her own urine levels reliably and regularly, by a process of training and feedback, and how to relate these levels to immediate dietary needs. There can also be training in how to recognize hyper- and hypoglycaemia even without the urine test.

Contribution to different client groups

The work of clinical and counselling psychologists varies considerably depending on the client groups that they work with. For example, in child and adolescent settings there is a greater emphasis on family interventions. In adult work, there is a special problem in dealing with long-term, chronic illness, especially schizophrenia, and how to maintain people with these problems in the community (Lavender & Holloway, 1988). In working with elderly people, one especially has to confront issues to do with the burden on relatives and carers. Those who work with people with learning difficulties have to tackle a whole range of challenging behaviours that stem from poor impulse control and delayed social learning. Psychologists working in health care have developed special interests in the role of health education and illness prevention. Even this brief list should dispel the notion that sitting face-to-face with a client is the only, or even the main, way of working. This important point is taken up again in the next part of the chapter.

PROFESSIONAL ISSUES

Range of roles

As just mentioned, there is a danger that in presenting models of therapy followed by strategies of treating merely a small sample of the great variety of problems posed by clients, groups of clients, or the system, that the impression will be created that face-to-face therapy contact is the primary kind of work. This is absolutely not the case. Psychologists work at a variety of levels. In addition to individual therapy, psychologists have an assessment role, particularly important in neuropsychology, to diagnose brain injury and impaired cognitive function; in childwork to assess cognitive development and specific cognitive defects; and in forensic work to assist in the placement of offenders. There is an immensely important training role, to "give away" intervention skills to parents, teachers, nurses, and so forth, so that the psychologist then acts as an adviser and source of support. Health education, especially to do with smoking, drug taking, AIDS, alcohol abuse, and heart disease, has an increasingly substantial role, involving the psychologist in issues of attitude change, social representation, health belief models, and advertising strategy. Many psychologists work not as individuals but as part of a team – community mental health teams working towards the placement of clients in community settings is just one example. Many psychologists now see no individual clients at all, but work entirely at the system level to improve strategies of health care and to design systems of service delivery. Other psychologists work primarily as researchers, developing fundamental knowledge, applying such knowledge in clinical settings within a research design, undertaking outcome research to determine efficacy and cost-effectiveness, and carrying out consumer research to see if the system is living up to its promises and aspirations.

Training

Training varies considerably between countries, but certainly in the USA and UK there are courses that are formally accredited; every few years they are revalidated by the American Psychological Association or the British Psychological Society, which hold lists of such approved courses. Training lasts usually for three years or more subsequent to a first degree in psychology. Training comprises a balance of supervised clinical work, academic study and research, and it is necessary to pass in all three areas. Training places are in great demand, and so it is often difficult to gain entrance without relevant experience and a very good academic record. Once on a course, the training is demanding because of the stressful nature of working with clients and the sheer breadth of material that has to be learned. However, there is a very wide diversity of employment opportunities available which enables graduates to pursue a career of great personal satisfaction.

Code of conduct

In order to protect clients, accredited psychologists (for example, "chartered" psychologists in the UK) are entered on to a register available to the public and are bound by a code of conduct. Registered, licensed, or chartered psychologists are expected to maintain and develop their professional competence and to work within its limits. They are not allowed to claim competence they do not possess, and are not allowed to make unjustifiable claims for the efficacy of their methods. They must preserve confidentiality in all its modalities, and conduct themselves in a manner not likely to damage their clients or the profession.

FURTHER READING

Barlow, D. H., Hayes, S. C., & Nelson, R. O. (1984). *The scientist practitioner*. New York: Pergamon.

Brewin, C. R. (1988). *Cognitive foundations of clinical psychology*. Hove: Lawrence Erlbaum.

Heppner, P. P., Kivlighan, D. M., Jr, & Wampold, B. E. (1992). *Research design in counseling*. Pacific Grove, CA: Brooks/Cole.

Lindsay, S. J. E., & Powell, G. E. (1987). *A handbook of clinical adult psychology* (3rd edn). Aldershot: Gower.

Patterson, C. H. (1986). *Theories of counseling and psychotherapy*. New York: Harper & Row.

REFERENCES

Adler, A. (1929). *Problems of neurosis*. New York: Harper & Row.

American Psychiatric Association (1987). *Diagnostic and statistical manual of mental disorders* (3rd edn, revised). Washington, DC: APA.

Bandura, A. (1969). *Principles of behavior modification*. New York: Holt, Rinehart & Winston.

Bandura, A. (1986). *Social foundations of thought and action: A social cognitive theory*. Englewood Cliffs, NJ: Prentice-Hall.

Barlow, D. H., Blanchard, E. B., Vermilyea, J. A., Vermilyea, B. B., & Di Nardo, P. A. (1986). Generalized anxiety and generalized anxiety disorder: Description and reconceptualization. *American Journal of Psychiatry*, *143*, 40–44.

Beck, A. T., Rush, A. J., Shaw, B. F., & Emery, G. (1977). *Cognitive therapy of depression*. New York: Guilford.

Brammer, L. M., Shostrom, E. L., & Abrego, P. J. (1989). *Therapeutic psychology: Fundamentals of counseling and psychotherapy* (5th edn). Englewood Cliffs, NJ: Prentice-Hall.

Creer, T. L. (1982). Asthma. *Journal of Consulting and Clinical Psychology*, *50*, 912–921.

Dobson, K. S. (1989). A meta-analysis of the efficacy of cognitive therapy for depression. *Journal of Consulting and Clinical Psychology*, *59*, 414–419.

Du Pont, R. L. (Ed.) (1982). *Phobias: A comprehensive summary of modern treatments*. New York: Brunner/Mazel.

Eagle, M. N. (1984). *Recent developments in psychoanalysis: A critical evaluation*. New York: McGraw-Hill.

Ellis, A., & Whiteley, J. M. (Eds) (1979). *Theoretical and empirical foundation of rational-emotive therapy*. Monterey, CA: Brooks/Cole.

Erikson, E. H. (1959). *Identity and the life cycle: Selected papers*. New York: International Universities Press.

Freud, S. (1943). *A general introduction to psychoanalysis*. New York: Garden City.

Garfield, S. L., & Bergin, A. E. (1986). *Handbook of psychotherapy and behavior change* (3rd edn). New York: Wiley.

Horowitz, M. J. (Ed.) (1988). *Psychodynamics and cognition*. Chicago, IL: University of Chicago Press.

Jacobson, N., & Gurman, A. (1986). *Clinical handbook of marital therapy*. New York: Guilford.

Jones, E. E., Kanouse, D. E., Kelley, H. H., Nisbett, P. E., Valins, S., & Weiner, B. (Eds) (1972). *Attribution: Perceiving the causes of behavior*. Morristown, NJ: General Learning Press.

Jung, C. G. (1982). *Contributions to analytical psychology*. New York: Harcourt Brace Jovanovich.

Kelly, G. A. (1955). *The psychology of personal constructs (vols 1 & 2)*. New York: Norton.

Klein, M. (1975). *Envy and gratitude and other works. 1946–1963*. London: Hogarth.

Laing, R. D. (1974). *The divided self*. Harmondsworth: Penguin.

Lavender, A., & Holloway, F. (Eds) (1988). *Community care in practice: Services for the continuing care client*. Chichester: Wiley.

Meichenbaum, D. (1977). *Cognitive behavior modification: An integrative approach*. New York: Plenum.

Minuchin, S., & Fishman, H. C. (1981). *Family therapy techniques*. Cambridge, MA: Harvard University Press.

Pavlov, I. P. (1927). *Conditioned reflexes. An investigation of the physiological activity of the cerebral cortex* (G. V. Anrep, ed. and trans.) Oxford: Oxford University Press (original work published 1923).

Perls, F. S. (1973). *The Gestalt approach*. Palo Alto, CA: Science and Behavior Books.

Powell, T. J., & Enright, S. J. (1990). *Anxiety and stress management*. London: Routledge.

Rogers, C. R. (1942). *Counseling and psychotherapy*. Boston, MA: Houghton Mifflin.

Skinner, B. F. (1974). *About behaviorism*. New York: Alfred A. Knopf.

Smith, M. L., Glass, G. V., & Miller, T. I. (1980). *The benefits of psychotherapy*. Baltimore, MD: Johns Hopkins University Press.

Spence, S. H. (1993). Interpersonal problems: Treatment. In S. Lindsay & G. E. Powell (Eds) *A handbook of clinical adult psychology* (pp. 240–255). London: Routledge.

Truax, C. B., & Carkhoff, R. (1967). *Toward effective counseling and psychotherapy: Training and practice*. Chicago, IL: Aldine.

Turner, S. M., & Beidel, D. C. (1988). *Treating obsessive-compulsive disorder*. New York: Pergamon.

2

EDUCATIONAL (SCHOOL) PSYCHOLOGY

David Fontana
University of Wales, Cardiff, Wales

The genesis of educational psychology	Pupil abilities
Developments from the 1950s to the 1970s	Affective factors
	The self and self-perceptions
	Child development
Developments in the 1980s and 1990s	Classroom interaction
	Teacher behaviour
Definition of educational psychology	Assessment
	How is it to be learned?
The content of educational psychology	**Other aspects of the educational psychologist's role**
What is to be learned?	**Conclusion: what more should educational psychology do?**
Educational objectives	
The importance of structure	**Further reading**
Who is to learn it?	**References**

The term *educational psychology* has traditionally covered two related but functionally distinct activities, first, the courses in psychology offered in the initial and continuing education of teachers, and second, the activities of psychologists whose main function is to assess children with learning and behaviour problems and make (or recommend) provision for their special educational needs. This dual terminology has led to some confusion; a partial solution has been to use *the psychology of education* to refer to the former activities, and *school psychology* to refer to the latter. However, there remains a clear need not only for more formalization in the use of these subgroup labels and in the generic term educational psychology, but also to ensure that all those offering services as educational psychologists have similar training and qualifications. Any understanding of the current role played by educational psychology demands that we keep in mind both uses of the term. However, both strands of educational psychology have their origin in a common source, as we shall see in an overview of the historical perspective of the subject.

THE GENESIS OF EDUCATIONAL PSYCHOLOGY

Educational psychology has an interesting and distinguished history (see, e.g., Child, 1985; Sutherland, 1985). Its formative influences can be traced to child psychology (e.g., the developmental norms established by authorities such as Gesell, together with the socio-emotional findings of McDougall, Goldfarb, Bowlby, and others), the study of mental testing (e.g., the work of Binet, Spearman, Thurstone, and Terman), psychodynamic psychology (in particular the writings of Freud and the neo- and post-Freudians), and the experimental investigation of human and animal learning (especially by pioneers like Pavlov, Watson, and Thorndike from behaviourism, and Kohler, Koffka, and Wertheimer from Gestalt psychology). Additional influences came from educational methods developed by non-psychologists such as Froebel and Montessori in continental Europe, Dewey in the USA, and the Macmillans and Susan Isaacs in the UK.

The formalization of these disparate influences into a subject worthy of the name of educational psychology owed much to the work of Sir Cyril Burt, who (in spite of the controversy surrounding his later experimental findings) did much to persuade both teachers and administrators of the crucial role that psychology can play in assessing children's educational needs and in informing classroom interaction. Over a long career stretching from 1912 (the date of his appointment by the London County Council in the first ever official post of educational psychologist) to his death in 1971, Burt remained a major influence on the subject, enjoying the respect of teachers and psychologists, through both his professional work (particularly his tenure of the Chair of Education in the University of London from 1931 to 1951) and his stream of publications.

Perhaps the main criticism that can be levelled at the general direction taken by educational psychology in these early years, however, is that it placed its emphasis primarily upon mental abilities and their assessment. From an initial concern to identify those children suffering from what were seen as mental disabilities, and who were consequently in need of special education and training, this emphasis soon spread to a more general attempt to test and categorize all children in terms predominantly of intelligence and of the verbal and spatial abilities of which intelligence was held to be composed.

Laudable enough in motive, since the expressed intention was to identify children with high potential abilities who were being under-served by the educational system, this emphasis not only tended to typecast children in terms of a somewhat simplistic mentalism, but also distracted attention from the range of other psychological factors that influence child behaviour and educational performance. In particular, it neglected social and affective factors, attitudes, motivation, self-concepts, classroom interaction, and teacher–child relationships. Furthermore, it placed undue stress upon the inheritance of mental abilities, and undue faith in the "scientific" nature of available mental tests. Arguably, the mistakes implicit in this approach, though long since discarded by educational psychology itself, remain as a potent influence on those responsible for educational policy and planning.

DEVELOPMENTS FROM THE 1950s TO THE 1970s

In the 1950s, 1960s, and 1970s, educational psychology became characterized by a much more child-centred approach, with the emphasis more upon the study of children's actual behaviour (both as individuals and as members of groups and subgroups) than upon the application of models of the mind or mental abilities. This change of emphasis was prompted by a number of factors, the most important of which will now be discussed.

First, there was the availability of new sources of psychological data with specific relevance to education, such as those from cognitive psychology (e.g., the work of Piaget, Bruner, and Vygotsky), personality theory (Allport, Erikson, and Maslow), psychometrics (Eysenck and Cattell), counselling and pastoral care (Rogers), and various approaches to learning theory and educational technology (Skinner, Gagné, Bloom, and Kelly).

Second, the increasing sophistication of research methods and techniques of statistical analysis greatly enhanced the database available within educational research.

Third, there were rapidly accumulating findings of sociology (particularly those relating to the family, ethnic groups, sub-cultures, and language), together with the greater awareness shown by society at large of the influence of social factors on child development and on educational opportunity and performance.

Finally, there was a portfolio of findings from across the whole spectrum of psychological research, including those produced by Harlow and Harlow on early attachment, Festinger on cognitive dissonance, Witkin, Kagan, and others on cognitive style, Guildford and others on creativity, McClelland on motivation, Kohlberg on moral development, Bandura on social learning, Rotter on locus of control, and Osgood on semantic space.

DEVELOPMENTS IN THE 1980s AND 1990s

With such a rich and varied field upon which to draw, and with the obvious relevance of educational psychology to classroom practice, it might be supposed that the 1980s and 1990s would see a major expansion of the influence and use of educational psychology. Unfortunately, within teacher education (the psychology of education), the subject is facing a major struggle both to retain its integrity as an identifiable domain and to be a major influence on classroom practice. Educational psychology has failed to demonstrate how the recommendations generated by psychological theory and research can be operationalized by the busy classteacher.

This failure in the view of many is a consequence of the dichtomy that developed during the 1970s within the teacher education curriculum between educational psychology and teaching method. Given the considerable amounts of specialist knowledge needed, it has proved increasingly difficult for any but a few exceptional individuals to be proficient in both areas, particularly when it comes to the preparation of teachers for work with older children. Tutoring in the two areas has therefore been carried out by specialists with different professional backgrounds, often working separately from each other. Thus the educational psychologist discusses children in isolation from the educational process, while the teaching methods tutor describes the educational process in isolation from the children who are its consumers. Where a team teaching approach has been adopted, the educational psychologist is usually reduced to a resource within the teaching methods curriculum, unable to teach the deep structure of educational psychology essential to a proper understanding of the discipline.

This erosion of educational psychology within teacher education has been exacerbated by the arrival of a number of hybrid subjects, each laying claim to some of its traditional territory. Educational technology and educational management have moved into such areas as learning, social relationships, and classroom control; special education (originally concerned primarily with teaching methods) has taken over work on individual needs; school effectiveness has appropriated work on social organization and assessment; and pastoral care has annexed work on psychological counselling. Extensive use is made of psychological knowledge in these areas, and qualified psychologists sometimes operate within them, but these are fields of study bidding to become disciplines in their own right, reducing educational psychology to what is effectively an auxiliary presence.

However, educational psychology has retained its importance in its second area of activity, the assessment of children with learning and behaviour problems (school psychology), primarily because it alone possesses expertise in the application and interpretation of the battery of diagnostic tests that such assessment demands. However, in face of the emphasis that modern industrial societies – for social and political as well as educational reasons – place upon assessment, educational (school) psychologists may well be manoeuvred into the role of psychological technicians, to the neglect of the other services that they are qualified to offer (discussed in more detail below).

DEFINITION OF EDUCATIONAL PSYCHOLOGY

Definitions are precarious things, often open to endless dispute and debate. However, a useful definition of educational psychology in both its *psychology of education* and *school psychology* roles is that it is, first, the study of those psychological factors that influence the educational process, and second, the development and application of psychological strategies in order to assist and where necessary improve this process. Like any scientific undertaking ("scientific" is used in its loosest sense — the social sciences cannot aspire to the precision of the natural sciences), educational psychology has a descriptive and an active function. It establishes *what is*, and then uses its methods and procedures to help bring about *what can be*. Both aspects are of equal importance; it is imperative that the first function, which involves well-conceived and meticulously executed fieldwork, does not become overshadowed by the second, with its perhaps more fashionable emphasis on the creation and testing of hypotheses.

THE CONTENT OF EDUCATIONAL PSYCHOLOGY

With the exception of the actual content of the school curriculum, educational psychology appears to cover virtually the whole of educational life, because education is about the very things (learning, child development, social relationships and interactions, assessment, motivation, social control, individual differences, and so on) that psychology claims for its own. Education is a psychological process, and much of our understanding of it comes from the findings of psychological research. Educational psychology is best grouped under a number of subheadings, which may suggest that it is a topic-driven subject, but this would be incorrect. One of the hallmarks of a discipline is that it carries a deep structure (referred to above) consisting of an interlaced framework of knowledge and methodology within which individual topics are recognized as points of emphasis rather than as discrete units. Thus each bears a clear relationship to the others and to the whole. Personality, for example, cannot be understood or sensibly taught without reference to learning; motivation without reference to self-concepts; social control without reference to social perceptions and social relationships; child development without reference to cognition; and so on. Thus the subheadings are simply a way of guiding the reader through the field, and should be interpreted only at this level. One useful way in which the various subheadings can themselves be grouped is to look at each of the three main interrelated questions with which the educational process is primarily concerned: What is to be learned? Who is to learn it? How is it to be learned?

26

WHAT IS TO BE LEARNED?

Decisions on what is to be included in the school curriculum for children of all ages and all abilities are not psychological decisions, but educational psychology has a great deal to say about how curriculum content should be presented to pupils if learning is to be optimized; this involves drawing attention to the importance of educational objectives and the deep structure of what is to be learned.

Educational objectives

In the mid-1950s, Bloom, Engelhart, Furst, Walker, and Krathwohl (1956) identified the general and specific categories that encompass all the learning outcomes that might be expected in the cognitive domain, while Krathwhol, Bloom, and Masie (1964) identified those in the affective domain, and Simpson (1972) those in the psycho-motor domain. The practical value of work of this kind is that it allows teachers to select and specify those aspects of curriculum content that are actually to be presented to pupils, and to monitor subsequently whether or not effective learning has taken place.

Wheldall has shown (e.g., Wheldall & Merrett, 1984, 1989) how the use of appropriate educational objectives not only can enhance the effectiveness with which classroom material is presented to pupils, but also can be readily accepted and used by teachers (see also Pearson & Tweddle, 1984). The precision teaching approach of Raybould (1984) is another example of how classroom material can be structured into a form which assists pupil understanding and learning. It is interesting to note how, outside the classroom, there is little doubt of the major contribution that the objectives approach can make to effective learning and behaviour (see, e.g., management training and practice – Seiwert, 1991).

The importance of structure

Bruner (1966) drew attention to the importance of organizing the material to be learned into a form that allows the pupil to recognize its deep structure, and to relate new information meaningfully to it. This calls for close cooperation between the educational psychologist and the teaching methods tutor so that the structure of classroom subjects can be properly identified and presented to pupils in a psychologically accessible form (i.e., one most suited to the ways in which individuals process incoming information and integrate it into existing cognitive structures).

The use of educational objectives is associated with the behavioural approach to human learning, while the identification and use of structure is related to the cognitive approach. These two approaches are sometimes seen as antipathetic to each other: it is important to point out that from the standpoint of educational psychology there is nothing contradictory about laying equal emphasis upon both. Structure identifies what needs to be learned, while objectives organize it into manageable units and make clear the whole point and purpose of the educational enterprise.

WHO IS TO LEARN IT?

This question brings us to the main focus of educational psychology, the children themselves. Under this heading comes the whole range of variables associated with child development, abilities and attainment, affective and social factors, and self-concepts and self-awareness. Given the long association of educational psychology with mental testing and child development, one might suppose that it has few problems either in identifying what teachers need to know about children, or in instructing teachers on how to make practical use of this knowledge within the classroom. However, this is not the case; the fault lies either with children themselves for being so complex, or with psychologists for being so pluralistic in their approach. Smith (1992) – to take a prime example – shows the conflict of opinion raging among psychologists over the quality and applicability of the research findings of Jean Piaget, previously the unquestioned authority on children's cognitive development. Other examples range from the classroom utility of personality trait theories to the long-term effects of early conditioning. Although the following are the main areas of psychology that have potential relevance to education, there is no consensus on how each of them can best be translated into classroom practice (a point to which I return in due course).

Pupil abilities

There is a whole range of variables within the individual which influence the efficacy of the learning act. Traditionally, psychology has assigned labels such as intelligence, creativity, memory, and motivation; of these, psychology has had most to say about intelligence. Yet even granted their validity, it is unclear how teachers can use psychological models of intelligence in their classroom work. Even a knowledge of children's test scores, however derived, is of doubtful practical value for most teachers, and can even be counter-productive (contributing, for example, to the well-known self-fulfilling prophecy). Unless educational psychology can make clear either how intelligence can be improved (if indeed it can), or how it relates directly to the way in which children learn, the situation (outside the assessment of children with special needs, dealt with below) is unlikely to change markedly.

Similarly with creativity: after the upsurge of interest shown by psychologists in the subject during the 1960s and 1970s, things have gone remarkably quiet, at least within the context of education. Various attempts have been made to demonstrate how teachers can enhance child creativity (e.g., Pickard, 1979), but many of these could equally well have been proposed by good art teachers or teachers of creative writing. Having set the stage, educational psychology failed to indicate the activities that should take place thereon.

Despite everything that psychology has to say about memory (e.g., Baddeley, 1983), for the average teacher a gap still yawns between the findings of psychological research and their application to classroom activities, while motivation, perhaps because it is so readily reduced to a few practical strategies (e.g., teaching through success rather than failure, through relevance and interest rather than through boredom, through intrinsic motivators as well as extrinsic) merely emphasizes what teachers already know. The relative impotence of educational psychology to make statements about individual abilities capable of greatly influencing day-to-day classroom practice may well be a reflection of the impotence of psychology itself. It could be argued that psychology has paid insufficient attention to human abilities in the normal population (particularly the normal population of older children), and to the ways in which these abilities influence behaviour and can be usefully enhanced.

Affective factors

Educational psychology embraces the ways in which affective factors influence both learning and the personal-social development of the child. A number of studies have used the personality measures of Eysenck and/or Catell and identified correlations between personality type and responses to the learning environment (Fontana, 1986); the pioneering work of Bennett (1976) was particularly notable in relation to the interaction between child personality and teaching styles. Within the personal-social development of the child, educational psychology has had to fight a battle against the traditional tendency of formal education to concentrate upon what I have referred to as an education for knowing rather than an education for being (Fontana, 1987). The overt curriculum has paid little more than lip-service to ways of helping children experience their lives and their relationships in a positive way, or for developing those qualities which psychologists equate with maturity of personality. A number of studies (e.g., Eisenberg & Strayer, 1987) make clear explicitly or by implication the scope possessed by the educational process to provide this kind of help, and the relevant skills, which educational psychology could make accessible to the classteacher.

Through its involvement in guidance, counselling, and pastoral care, educational psychology can also provide practical strategies for identifying and helping children with personality and/or social problems (Murphy and Kupshik, 1992; Nelson-Jones, 1986). Although not normally regarded as its direct concern, educational psychology can also assist in careers counselling (Ball, 1984).

The self and self-perceptions

Linked to both cognitive and affective factors, the child's view of him- or herself can be a crucial variable in both formal classroom learning and personal development (Burns, 1982). There is no shortage of psychological material on the self and the growth of self-awareness (Kegan, 1982); Burns (among others) has shown how much of this material can be suitably operationalized within education (Burns, 1982). If there is a resistance to progress here, it comes more from formal education, with its lack of proper concern for an education for personal development, than from any lack of knowledge within educational psychology.

Child development

Child development is a vast, well-researched subject within psychology (Bee, 1989; Kagan, 1984); although marked by pluralism (mention has been made of the debate surrounding Piaget's experimental findings), major areas are relevant to education (see, e.g., Branthwaite & Rogers, 1985). It is perhaps unfortunate that psychology has concentrated more on early childhood than on adolescence – the developmental stage that occasions teachers most heartache – but educational psychology is replete with knowledge of the many, subtle ways in which development influences a child's ability to learn, to relate to others, and to grow in self-awareness. Across a spectrum of topics, including the development of perception, cognition, social identity and relationships, language, moral behaviour, play, personality, psychosexuality, and creative abilities, educational psychologists could make this knowledge available to teachers in a form that has direct impact upon the way in which they understand and relate to children (see, e.g., Desforges, 1989; Fontana, 1984a, 1984b; Hartley, 1985; Stubbs, 1983).

Classroom interaction

The analysis of classroom interaction has been of interest both to educational psychology and to educational sociology (Delamont, 1983), as it identifies the incidents during teacher–child interactions that effect significant changes in children's behaviour (and less obviously in their cognitive and affective processes) in both desirable and undesirable directions. Such changes have important implications for children's learning and for the teacher's ability to maintain classroom control; since the introduction in 1970 of properly constructed instruments for recording and analysing this interaction (Flanders,

1970) student teachers have been able to learn a great deal about the consequences of their own classroom behaviour (see, e.g., Bennett, 1985). The findings from both interaction analysis and cognitive and behavioural psychology have enabled educational psychology to advise more fully on classroom management (Laslett & Smith, 1984) and classroom control and discipline (Fontana, 1985; Wheldall, 1992).

Teacher behaviour

Teacher behaviour is another area where educational psychology links closely with work on teaching method. The aim of both educational psychologists and teaching method tutors is to enhance teacher effectiveness in the presentation of the learning act and in classroom management and control (referred to above). Educational psychology also attempts to help teachers identify those psychological variables within themselves that contribute towards professional success. Longitudinal studies (e.g., Cortis, 1985) have drawn attention to these variables, while work on teacher stress (Cole & Walker, 1990; Greenberg, 1984) has helped furnish educational psychology with a range of stress-reducing strategies available for use in in-service teacher education (Fontana, 1989).

Assessment

The detailed assessment (or screening) of children with special educational needs is central to the function of educational psychologists engaged in school psychology. The assessment tests used (which include structured and unstructured interviews, time-sampling, classroom observation, and verbal and written tests) are so varied, with many having been developed in response to specific needs, that it would be impossible to list them all here. Together they cover the major categories as follows:

1 *learning difficulties* e.g., numeracy, literacy, reasoning, language, and memory tests
2 *sensory impairment* e.g., visual, speech, and auditory tests
3 *physical impairment* e.g., tests for motor handicap, laterality problems, and physical injury
4 *behaviour difficulties* e.g., observation and interviews for hyperactivity, aggression, delinquent acts, school refusal, and truancy
5 *emotional problems* e.g., tests for anxiety, personality difficulties, withdrawal, and fantasizing.

In the application and interpretation of various tests and measures, the educational psychologist will often work with other child and health-care specialists such as doctors, physiotherapists, and social workers. On completion of testing, the educational psychologist presents the results to the educational authorities and (where required) to the parents, and offers recommendations as to the kind of educational provision that the child may need. This could consist of remedial help within the child's own school or (more rarely) transfer to a school specially equipped to cater for his or her special requirements.

The age at which children are first screened for special needs depends on both the child and the policy of the educational psychologists concerned. It is generally felt inappropriate (and often impossible in practice, since they may not have entered formal schooling) to screen children before they are 5 or 6 years old. Screening before this age often proves unreliable, as psychological development in young children tends to be uneven, and the children may refuse to cooperate with the tester. Furthermore, early screening carries the risk that the child will be labelled in the eyes of parents and teachers, and become the victim of a self-fulfilling prophecy. However, if screening is left too late, it simply confirms that the child is having educational difficulties, instead of identifying his or her problems before these difficulties have a chance to arise.

HOW IS IT TO BE LEARNED?

Learning is the prime concern of both psychology and education, and should be the area on which educational psychology speaks with most authority. Although both behavioural and cognitive theories of learning have obvious relevance to our understanding of the way in which children approach and perform the learning act, it is less clear that a knowledge of them is a significant stimulus to good practice. It is unclear whether a teacher who is familiar with these theories is a more successful (or even a markedly different) practitioner from one who is not. This is why many educational psychologists involved in teacher education currently doubt the efficacy of their own subject (see, e.g., Burden, 1992; Tomlinson, 1992; for an examination of some of the issues being raised). However, the problem lies not in the failure of psychological knowledge, but in the absence of consensus on how this knowledge translates into good classroom practice. This lack of consensus is puzzling, given the various authoritative texts addressing the issue (e.g., Bigge, 1982; Fontana, 1984a, 1988; Gronlund, 1978; Howe, 1984; Wheldall & Merritt, 1989), and in view of the evidence that educational psychologists working alongside serving teachers can initiate them into the use of psychological strategies that can materially assist them in their task (Thacker, 1990).

In addition, current work in repertory grids, computer-assisted learning, and self-organized learning (Thomas & Harri-Augstein, 1985), on peer-tutoring (Foot, Morgan, & Schute, 1990) and on how to relate learning to evolving models of mind (Claxton, 1990) provides not only a major stimulus for new thinking in educational psychology, but also an array of practical strategies which most teachers find no difficulty in learning, enjoying, and applying. The debate among educational psychologists on how best to help teachers understand and apply a useful and practical psychology of learning would seem to have more to do with their own uncertainty about their professional role than to any lack of material suitable for the task concerned.

OTHER ASPECTS OF THE EDUCATIONAL PSYCHOLOGIST'S ROLE

Educational psychologists are equipped by their training and experience to undertake a number of functions (in addition to those mentioned above), and can work effectively in any situation involving not only formal and informal education but also the processes of human change and development. They may work in psychological counselling, primarily with children and also on occasions with adults; their duties frequently include child guidance and working alongside teachers in schools to develop counselling and pastoral care networks. With additional training, they may practise psychotherapy with a wide range of disorders, including social and emotional problems, eating problems, anxieties and phobias, and low self-esteem.

In family work, skills range from simple advice to parents on appropriate child-rearing practices to in-depth family therapy work. Educational psychologists may work with groups of children and adolescents to assist the development of social competence and human relationship skills, and with groups of teachers and other professionals to offer guidance on stress management, study skills, classroom control, and child assessment.

Educational psychologists may advise on organizational matters, on the running and management of a school, on appropriate channels of communication, and in the general area of school effectiveness. Many educational psychologists carry out research, often linking up with developmental, clinical, and social psychologists. They may also work in teams with creative arts therapists, such as drama and music therapists, and with allied professionals such as social workers and community care agents.

CONCLUSION: WHAT MORE SHOULD EDUCATIONAL PSYCHOLOGY DO?

The future of educational psychology is intimately bound up with the future both of psychology and of education. Educational psychologists are concerned with the professional training of specific groups of students if they are involved in *the psychology of education*, and with specific duties in connection with schools if they are engaged in *school psychology*. Changes in the content or structure of teacher education will have repercussions on their work, as will changes in school policy consequent upon the actions of national and local politicians.

Educational psychology is not entirely at the mercy of factors beyond its control, however. There is a need for it to assert its own identity more clearly within both psychology and education: the time has come for it to play a role in urging the need for more attention and resources to be devoted to applied educational psychology. Non-psychologists expect psychology to provide insights that relate directly to personal and professional life. Educational psychology is primarily an applied exercise: as such, it has much to teach the parent discipline of psychology. It needs to assert more clearly the psychological content of education, and the fact that education cannot be fully understood and conducted without appropriate psychological knowledge.

Teaching cannot be a fully effective exercise unless the teacher understands and can apply the psychological elements involved in the three interrelated educational questions: *What is to be learned? What is to learn it? How is it to be learned?* The best setting in which to make this plain is the classroom itself, working alongside serving teachers. Within the classroom, teachers can be taught by the educational psychologist to operate as researchers, capable of monitoring their own behaviour, together with that of the children, in order to identify where psychological factors are hindering learning or personal-social development, and where changes in strategy are therefore needed.

This is not to deny the place for a study of educational psychology by student teachers in the lecture room, and by serving teachers on in-service training courses. No profession (e.g., medicine, engineering, law, or dentistry) would pretend that students or serving professionals can do all their learning while on task. Various attempts have been made to set out the major areas to be studied in college-based educational psychology courses, while comprehensive textbooks also exist (see below). But it is within the school setting that educational psychology can most emphatically demonstrate its value. And it is within the school setting that it must in the future seek fully to demonstrate its worth.

FURTHER READING

Bennett, N., & Desforges, C. (1985). *Recent advances in classroom research*. Edinburgh: Scottish Academic Press and British Journal of Educational Psychology.

Fontana, D. (1988). *Psychology for teachers* (2nd edn). London: British Psychological Society and Macmillan.

Francis, H. (Ed.) (1985). *Learning to teach: Psychology in teacher training*. London: Falmer.

Jones, N., & Frederickson, N. (Eds) (1990). *Refocusing educational psychology*. Basingstoke: Falmer.

REFERENCES

Baddeley, A. (1983). *Your memory: A user's guide*. Harmondsworth: Penguin.

Ball, B. (1984). *Careers counselling in practice*. London: Falmer.

Bee, H. (1989). *The developing child* (5th edn). New York: Harper & Row.

Bennett, N. (1976). *Teaching styles and pupil progress*. London: Open Books.

Bennett, N. (1985). Interaction and achievement in classroom groups. In N. Bennett & C. Desforges (Eds) *Recent advances in classroom research* (pp. 105–119). Edinburgh: Scottish Academic Press and British Journal of Educational Psychology.

Bigge, N. (1982). *Learning theories for teachers* (4th edn). New York: Harper & Row.

Bloom, B. S., Engelhart, M. D., Furst, E. J., Walker, M. H., & Krathwohl, D. R. (1956). *Taxonomy of educational objectives*. London: Longmans Green.

Branthwaite, A., & Rogers, D. (Eds) (1985). *Children growing up*. Milton Keynes: Open University Press.

Bruner, J. S. (1966). *Towards a theory of instruction*. New York: Norton.

Burden, R. (1992). Educational psychology: A force that is spent or one that never got going? *The Psychologist, 5*(3), 110–111.

Burns, R. (1982). *Self-concept development and education*. London: Holt, Rinehart & Winston.

Child, D. (1985). Educational psychology, past, present and future. In N. J. Entwistle (Ed.) *New directions in educational psychology: I. Learning and teaching* (pp. 9–24). London: Falmer.

Claxton, G. (1990). *Teaching to learn: A direction for education*. London: Cassell.

Cole, M., & Walker, S. (Eds) (1990). *Teaching and stress*. Milton Keynes: Open University Press.

Cortis, G. A. (1985). Eighteen years on: How far can you go? *Educational Review, 37*(1), 3–12.

Delamont, S. (1983). *Interaction in the classroom* (2nd edn). London: Methuen.

Desforges, C. (Ed.) (1989). *Early childhood education*. Edinburgh: Scottish Academic Press and British Journal of Educational Psychology.

Eisenberg, N., & Strayer, J. (Eds) (1987). *Empathy and its development*. Cambridge: Cambridge University Press.

Flanders, N. A. (1970). *Analyzing teaching behavior*. New York: Addison-Wesley.

Fontana, D. (Ed.) (1984a). *Behaviourism and learning theory in education*. Edinburgh: Scottish Academic Press and British Journal of Educational Psychology.

Fontana, D. (Ed.) (1984b). *The education of the young child* (2nd edn). Oxford: Basil Blackwell.

Fontana, D. (1985). *Classroom control: Understanding and guiding classroom behaviour*. London: Methuen and British Psychological Society.

Fontana, D. (1986). *Teaching and personality* (2nd edn). Oxford: Basil Blackwell.

Fontana, D. (1987). Knowing about being. *Changes, 5*, 344–347.

Fontana, D. (1988). *Psychology for teachers* (2nd edn). London: Macmillan and British Psychological Society.

Fontana, D. (1989). *Managing stress*. London: Routledge and British Psychological Society.

Foot, H., Morgan, M., & Schute, R. (1990). *Children helping children*. Chichester: Wiley.

Greenberg, S. F. (1984). *Stress and the teaching profession*. London: Paul Brooks.

Gronlund, N. E. R. (1978). *Stating objectives for classroom instruction* (2nd edn). London: Collier Macmillan.

Hartley, J. (1985). Developing skills in learning. In A. Branthwaite & D. Rogers (Eds) *Children growing up* (pp. 112–121). Milton Keynes: Open University Press.

Howe, M. J. (1984). *A teacher's guide to the psychology of learning*. Oxford: Basil Blackwell.

Kagan, J. (1984). *The nature of the child*. New York: Harper & Row.

Kegan, R. (1982). *The evolving self: Problems and process in human development*. Cambridge, MA: Massachusetts University Press.

Krathwohl, D. R., Bloom, B. S., & Masie, B. B. (1964). *Taxonomy of educational objectives: Handbook II. The affective domain*. New York: David McKay.

Laslett, R., & Smith, C. (1984). *Effective classroom management*. London: Croom Helm.

Lindsay, G. (Ed.) (1984). *Screening for children with special needs*. London: Croom Helm.

Murphy, P. M., & Kupshik, G. A. (1992). *Loneliness, stress and well-being: A helper's guide*. London: Routledge.

Nelson-Jones, R. (1986). *Human relationship skills: Training and self-help*. London: Cassell.

Pearson, L., & Tweddle, D. (1984). The formulation and use of behavioural objectives. In D. Fontana (Ed.) *Behaviourism and learning theory in education* (pp. 75–92). Edinburgh: Scottish Academic Press and British Journal of Educational Psychology.

Pickard, E. (1979). *Development of creative ability*. Slough: National Foundation for Educational Research.

Raybould, E. C. (1984). Precision teaching and pupils with learning difficulties: Perspectives, principles and practice. In D. Fontana (Ed.) *Behaviourism and learning theory in education* (pp. 43–74). Edinburgh: Scottish Academic Press and British Journal of Educational Psychology.

Seiwert, L. (1991). *Time in money*. London: Kogan Page.

Simpson, E. J. (1972). *The classification of educational objectives in the psychomotor domain*. Washington, DC: Gryphon.

Smith, L. (1992). *Jean Piaget: Critical assessments*, 4 vols. London: Routledge.

Stubbs, M. (1983). *Language, schools and classrooms* (2nd edn). London: Methuen.

Sutherland, M. B. (1985). Psychology and the education of teachers. In H. Francis (Ed) *Learning to teach: Psychology in teacher training* (pp. 6–21). London: Falmer.

Thacker, V. J. (1990). Working through groups in the classroom. In N. Jones & N. Frederickson (Eds) *Refocusing educational psychology* (pp. 8–83). Basingstoke: Falmer.

Thomas, L., & Harris-Augstein, S. (1985). *Self-organised learning*. London: Routledge & Kegan Paul.

Tomlinson, P. (1992). Psychology and education: What went wrong – or did it? *The Psychologist*, 5(3), 105–109.

Wheldall, K. (Ed.) (1992). *Discipline in schools: Psychological perspectives on the Elton Report*. London: Routledge.

Wheldall, K., & Merrett, F. (1984). The behavioural approach to classroom management. In D. Fontana (Ed.) *Behaviourism and learning theory in education* (pp. 15–42). Edinburgh: Scottish Academic Press and British Journal of Educational Psychology.

Wheldall, K., & Merrett, F. (1989). *Positive teaching in the secondary school*. London: Paul Chapman.

3

INDUSTRIAL (OCCUPATIONAL) AND ORGANIZATIONAL PSYCHOLOGY

Wendy Hollway

University of Bradford, England

Labels and their origins	**Human relations**
Scientific management and the	**Conclusion**
task idea	**Further reading**
Human factors	**References**
Selection	

The subject first emerged as *industrial psychology* in the early years of the twentieth century. In Britain, it came to be known as *occupational psychology*. Following broader trends in social science, the title *organizational psychology* has emerged for a sibling subject with less of a focus on the individual. *Work psychology* is a term used in continental Europe, but only just appearing in Britain and unfamiliar in the United States. It is used in this chapter, to avoid the historical and geographical specificity of the terms contained in the title, when it is necessary to refer to the topic in a general way.

Work psychology applies psychology in the workplace. It sounds simple and clear-cut: there is a scientific body of knowledge about the individual called psychology and in this branch it is applied to the study of individuals at work. In this chapter I point out the deficiencies of this definition, emphasizing in contrast the effects of workplace practices in the production of knowledge about people at work.

The present-day *Journal of Occupational Psychology* (subtitled "an

International Journal of Industrial and Organizational Psychology") defines its subject matter as follows:

> The journal's domain is broad, covering industrial, organizational, engineering, vocational and personnel psychology, as well as behavioural aspects of industrial relations, ergonomics, human factors and industrial sociology. Interdisciplinary approaches are welcome. (Guide notes for referees)

Managers, not psychologists, are the largest group who practise, and are trained in, work psychology (Shimmin & Wallis, 1989). Other practitioners who often have some training in work psychology are consultants, trainers, and researchers (few of whom would carry the label "psychologist"). They are employed by organizations to do the following:

1 help select employees
2 devise appraisal systems
3 design systems and methods of work organization
4 instigate change in the organization
5 advise on the introduction of new technology
6 advise on personnel planning and succession plans
7 enhance safety
8 enhance productivity
9 cope with stress and conflict
10 help to problem solve
11 improve decision-making and team-work
12 find out what employees think about their jobs and about the company
13 negotiate pay and conditions
14 counsel people when they lose their jobs
15 advise people on what jobs suit them and how to create a favourable impression on application
16 train managers to manage people and supervisors to supervise them in ways that will promote a climate favourable to the work of the organization.

The list is impressive in its diversity; what the items have in common is that they require knowledge about how people work, for the purpose of improving it.

As is evident from this list, the problems and practices concerning the regulation of people at work are diverse and not shaped by conventional categories of psychology. None the less, they have been influential in defining what work psychology is: in this they have been more influential than the discipline of psychology has been. Indeed, where psychology had little relevant to offer, as in the case of motivation theory (Hollway, 1991, pp. 8–10 and chap. 6), the practical problems of motivating people at work led to an unrelated body of motivation theory which is particular to work psychology (Herzberg, 1968; Herzberg, Mausner, & Snyderman, 1959; McClelland, 1961).

Three questions will protect readers from uncritically accepting the over-simplified definition of work psychology with which this chapter began. First, what does being scientific mean in the context of application, and does it provide the guarantees that science implies? Second, to what end, and on whose behalf, do psychologists study individuals at work, and what effects do they have? Is the purpose to enable them to be happier workers, or better workers? Is it primarily on behalf of the employee or the management? Efficiency or welfare, or both? Third, what were the conditions for the emergence of the various strands of work psychology?

I start with a historical approach to the different labels, which gives insight into the changes in the discipline since the early 1920s and reminds us that work psychology is not a consistent, coherent body of knowledge, but a pragmatic amalgam without clear boundaries of potentially useful approaches to a practical problem: the regulation of the individual at work. The other two questions provide themes which run through this chapter and to which I return at the end.

LABELS AND THEIR ORIGINS

When the subject first emerged as industrial psychology after the First World War, it was rather different in character in Britain and the United States. Prior to that war, the practical space into which industrial psychology was to enter was dominated by scientific management (see below). Industrial psychology's focus is on the individual worker, and because scientific management was the first discourse systematically to target the individual worker, industrial psychology claims F. W. Taylor as its forefather and sometimes as its founding father. Although scientific management had profound effects on management practice in Europe (Devinat, 1927) and in Britain ("Some Principles of Industrial Organization ... "), it was most influential in the United States, its birthplace (Hoxie, 1915).

In Britain, industrial psychology was launched on the reputation of fatigue research (see below), which seemed to promote both industrial welfare and industrial efficiency. The method was experimental and the perspective psychophysiological (Myers, 1926). This approach was also termed *human factors*. In the United States and Germany the initial paradigm was the same, borrowing the dominant experimental method and psychophysiological perspective from the emerging scientific psychology. In 1932 in Britain the *Journal of the National Institute of Industrial Psychology (JNIIP)* changed its name to *Human Factors*. In 1938 it was changed again to *Occupational Psychology* in order that "its coverage should be even wider than that suggested by the adjective 'industrial'" (Rodger, 1972). Charles Myers, the head of the NIIP, wanted the *JNIIP* to be concerned with "psychological problems arising in work of every kind and every level in organizations of every sort and every size" (Rodger, 1972). Out of line with the rest of the western world, "occupational psychology" remains the accepted title in Britain, although there has been a debate about changing the title of the *Journal of Occupational Psychology* (Occupational Psychology Section and Division joint meeting 1990, p. 375).

A consensual definition in British occupational psychology for several decades, until the influx of human relations approaches in the 1970s, was the one given by the first British professor of Occupational Psychology, Alec Rodger. It was concerned with

> practical and theoretical problems arising from "fitting the man to the job" (through vocational guidance, personnel selection and occupational training) and "fitting the job to the man" (through methods development, equipment design and layout, and the arrangement of working conditions and rewards. (Birkbeck College, 1961, describing the new postgraduate department in Occupational Psychology)

Thus it became known as the FMJ–FJM approach (fitting the man to the job – fitting the job to the man).

In the United States, the use of psychometric testing to place over 1 million personnel in the armed services changed the course of industrial psychology almost at the outset to a discipline where psychological measurement provided the method and the psychology of individual differences provided the perspective. This tradition, which has no theoretical or methodological base in common with human factors, was before long the dominant practice of industrial psychology. It has retained the status of the "jewel in the crown" of work psychology and since the early 1980s has renewed its position of dominance as the influence of human relations psychology has declined. The specific field is sometimes referred to as personnel psychology (more commonly in the USA) or vocational psychology. Whereas personnel psychology reflects the point of view of the employer interested in selection, placement, and promotion, vocational psychology has been applied both to this and to the individual, often school-leaver, deciding on the kind of work she or he would like to do.

Starting in the 1920s in the United States, the Hawthorne research (discussed below) was applying new socio-psychological approaches to address problems of worker satisfaction in machine-paced jobs. This was the beginning of the human relations paradigm, which still underpins "organizational behaviour". Organizational behaviour (OB) is an initially American label for a human-relations-based subject allied to work psychology, using neither laboratory experiment nor psychometrics, which attempts an organizational and socio-emotional perspective on its subject (Hollway, 1991, pp. 109ff). In Britain, OB owes more to a "scientific" social-psychological tradition. Organizational psychology is that part of OB, the greater part, which is not sociology.

Work psychology can be placed in relationship to a number of adjoining disciplines. At the social end, industrial sociology overlaps with organizational behaviour. At the physiological end, ergonomics overlaps with industrial psychology, through the psycho-physiological, experimental tradition. According to the British Ergonomics Research Society, ergonomics is the study of the relation between humans and their occupation, equipment, and environment, and particularly the application of anatomical, physiological, and psychological knowledge to problems arising therefrom (Shackel, 1974).

In the United States, industrial psychology and human relations or organizational behaviour have existed relatively independently of each other, the latter being fraternized by a majority of non-psychologists and identified with management ideas. In the expansion of the 1970s, human relations principles infiltrated eventually into British occupational psychology where they cohabited uncomfortably with the scientific tradition. Since much of occupational psychology was practised by non-psychologists and there was no career path and there were few specific jobs for occupational psychologists as such, the demands of the market (for students, consultancy, and research grants) dictated that human relations paradigms be accepted into work psychology. Organization development (OD) became a high-profile and attractive area for work psychologists.

In the recessions of the 1980s the trend reversed back to a dependence on work psychology's core skill of psychometrics. Instead of developing their middle and senior level staff through expensive human relations programmes, organizations were interested in selecting them correctly in the first place. In Britain and the rest of Europe, following the American trend, there was a spectacular growth of small commercial companies whose primary stock-in-trade was psychological measurement (Shimmin & Wallis, 1989). Since many of the central tests used in personnel selection are restricted to qualified users, these companies wanted qualified psychologists. In addition, these psychologists might be expected to perform most of the activities listed at the beginning of this chapter.

Work psychology has thrived by mingling with management training, human resource development, and personnel management. In the current climate, where psychological practice is subject to professional regulation, this poses a dilemma: who is allowed to practise what? It is impossible and undesirable for psychologists to control most of the practices concerning the regulation of the individual at work. Psychometric testing, however, is restricted, and this has confirmed its place as the core of work psychology.

I shall now trace the development of the different discourses within work psychology, starting with the conditions for the emergence of industrial psychology in the first decades of the twentieth century.

SCIENTIFIC MANAGEMENT AND THE TASK IDEA

Scientific management in its widest sense refers to the attempts made to devise efficient systems of industrial production and organization. In its narrower sense, it refers to the specific principles advocated by the US engineer F. W. Taylor before the First World War. Taylor's aim was increased productivity and the elimination of waste through management control of the labour process: "As to the importance of obtaining the maximum output of each man and each machine, it is only through the adoption of modern scientific management that this great problem can be finally solved" (Taylor, 1967, p. 27).

Three areas of scientific management became the province of industrial psychology: training workers in new methods devised by management; design of tools; and selection. The task idea, "the most prominent single element in modern scientific management" (Taylor, 1967, p. 64), meant that "the task of every workman is fully planned out, and each man usually receives written instructions describing in the minutest detail the work which he is to accomplish, as well as the means to be used in doing it" (Cadbury, 1914, p. 101). The task idea is significant for the emergence of management and for industrial psychology in two ways: its object was the individual worker, and it systematized the removal of autonomy from the workforce and transferred knowledge and further control into the hands of management.

Industrialization established the ground for management to emerge: increasingly the machinery developed for production necessitated the containment of labour in factories, rather than the old system of "putting out". Partly governed by the new machinery and partly by the desire to limit workers' control over their work, jobs became narrow, specialized, and stripped of the craft skill previously associated with them.

The deskilling of labour produced a new management class to deal with a problem of control which has been fundamental to the history of western capitalism and of industrial psychology. In the mid-nineteenth century in the United States, there were no middle managers. Fifty years later, management was well established with its own training institutions and journals: "Rarely in the history of the world has an institution grown to be so important and so pervasive in so short a period of time" (Chandler, 1977, p. 4).

Scientific management claimed that, through the task idea, industry would become more productive and trouble-free as it "gathers up, systematizes and systematically transmits to the workers all the traditional craft knowledge and skill which is being lost and destroyed under current industrial methods" (Taylor, quoted in Hoxie, 1915, p. 10). In effect this was a transfer of control from workers to management and was a significant part of the creation of management. To set the task, and to control it, management had to transfer all the specific knowledge and skill required to do particular jobs into its own hands.

The task idea is significant for a second major reason: it provided an industrial relations strategy which changed the focus from workers en masse (the response to which was unionization) to workers as individuals. This shift of focus to regulation of the individual worker was an essential condition of the emergence of industrial psychology, as well as being a political tool to counter increasing organization of labour into trade unions.

Scientific management also prepared the ground for industrial psychology by offering the means for workplace discipline to shift from the reign of arbitrary personal authority to the rule of law, procedure, and science. In Taylor's discourse (consistent with the wider status of natural science at the time), science functions as the neutral arbiter, outside the interests both of management and labour. The appeal to science denies power relations, since it produces "natural" laws which management too must observe: "It substitutes joint obedience of employers and workers to fact and law for obedience to personal authority" (Taylor, quoted in Hoxie, 1915, p. 9). Although science is supposedly the neutral arbiter, in practice "every protest of every workman must be handled by those on management side" (ibid). This "science" was produced on behalf of management.

Scientific management did not achieve the desired social regulation. With the destruction of the craft tradition and the introduction of machine-paced jobs, the control of the workforce became an issue of the utmost importance to employers. Absenteeism, restriction of output, and sabotage were rampant, even though supervision reached marathon proportions (Goldman & van Houten, 1979).

Scientific management targeted the individual as the problem of control, but since it stripped workers of any vestige of responsibility for their own work and yet failed to curb the foreman's arbitrary personal authority (for example Mayo, quoted in Hollway, 1991, p. 82), it exacerbated the problem. It required the counselling and interpersonal skills training programmes at the Hawthorne works to tackle the arbitrary authority of the foreman (Hollway, 1991, chap. 5). In this sense, scientific management ushered in human relations, which grew and became influential on the basis of its claim to get workers to regulate themselves. The concepts of motivation, job satisfaction, interpersonal skills for managers, and the long-running attempt at democratic leadership style, all testify to the shift from coercion of bodies to the attempted production of self-regulated individuals in managerial knowledge and practice. The primary problem still being addressed by contemporary work psychology is how to place responsibility for the work back in the hands of the worker. Whereas quantity could be partly regulated by the production line, quality has continued to evade supervision.

The greater strength of trade unions in Britain was an important factor in the take-up of scientific management, in regard both to its extent and emphasis. In the eyes of progressive British employers, the sorts of exploitation that were attributed to scientific management in the United States would court industrial unrest and possibly revolution in Britain:

The reduction of the workman to a living tool, with differential bonus schemes to induce him to expend his last ounce of energy, while initiative and judgement and freedom of movement are eliminated, in the long run must either demoralise the workman, or more likely in England, produce great resentment and result in serious differences between masters and men. (Cadbury, 1914, p. 105)

Industrial psychology in Britain emerged in close cooperation with the industrial welfare movement, that is, with progressive employers who had learned that it was necessary not to antagonize organized workers (Hollway, 1993).

HUMAN FACTORS

The problem of fatigue became prominent in the British munitions industry during the First World War, where the productivity of workers was improved at the same time as reducing hours of work and introducing improvements in working conditions.

During the nineteenth century, industrial workers organized to combat excruciatingly long hours; however, no attention was paid to the relation of hours to productivity. Workers were regarded as "hands", and from this perspective, employers assumed that the more hours they were put to work, the more they would produce. It took the conditions of war, and the reputation of science, to produce a wider acceptance of the principle that longer hours did not necessarily mean greater output.

Trade union organization, industrial unrest, and government response in the form of legislation on hours and working conditions, had succeeded in reducing working hours dramatically by the First World War. Then hours were increased to 70–90 a week, over 90 hours being not infrequent (Hearnshaw & Winterbourn, 1945). Studies showed the advantage in reduced hours: "In one investigation concerned with the heavy work of sizing fuse bodies, reducing the hours worked from 58.2 per week to 51.2 resulted in an increased total output of 22 percent. The hourly output increased from 100 to 139" (Hearnshaw & Winterbourn, 1945, p. 22). The findings of the wartime fatigue studies can be summarized as follows:

An extension of the usual hours of work does not – except for short periods during an emergency – give a proportional increase of output; on the contrary it causes the rate of output to fall off with increasing rapidity. . . . After a continuous period of overtime, improvement in output rate does not take place for some time after the re-introduction of shorter hours. . . . An unbroken spell of four and a half to five hours is generally too long. Man must rest even at work. (Industrial Health Research Board, 1940, quoted in Hearnshaw & Winterbourn, 1945, pp. 22–24)

The question of fatigue united concerns that were already of political importance: national efficiency, the health of the labouring classes and, because of trade union demands, working conditions in factories.

Psychologists were able to take much of the credit for this noteworthy achievement of advancing the goals of efficiency and welfare simultaneously (Mansion House meeting, 1922, p. 60) and it was on the basis of this reputation that psychology claimed a useful place in British industry and, in 1921, established the National Institute of Industrial Psychology (NIIP), an independent, self-financing organization, supported by politicians and progressive employers.

At one of its early fund-raising events in London, the aims of the NIIP were summarized in a speech as

> to assist employers in finding the best way to do each piece of work by the aid of scientific knowledge and scientific methods; and in addition to finding the best way to do each piece of work, we also want to help the employer to find the best job for each worker. (Mansion House meeting, 1922, p. 60)

None the less, industrial psychology was associated by many with scientific management, efficiency engineering, and "speeding up":

> It was obvious that the workers were straightway prejudiced against it by such terms as "efficiency" and "scientific management". By improvement in efficiency they feared speeding-up and the dismissal of their less competent comrades. The mention of scientific management made them suspect that all their craft knowledge would pass from them into the hands of their employers and that they would be degraded to the position of servile mechanisms. (Myers, 1926, p. 26)

Myers distinguished industrial psychology from efficiency engineering in the following way:

> It was sought not to press the worker from behind, but to ease the difficulties which may confront him. It has aimed at removing the obstacles which prevent the worker from giving his best to the work and it has almost invariably succeeded in increasing output by this method. (ibid., p. 28)

A report by consultants from an NIIP team who worked on contract for Rowntree's Cocoa Works before it established a Psychological Department provides an example of this approach:

> Under the new method here described, output increased by over 35% and the workers were unanimous in their appreciation of a considerable saving of fatigue at the end of the day, spontaneously expressing to the investigators their gratitude. (Farmer & Eyre, 1922, p. 12)

Psychologists in the human factors tradition are reputed for their meticulous scientific study of working conditions (Shimmin, 1986). However, the NIIP became increasingly dependent on work based on psychometric testing which employers wanted in order to improve selection. There was a retreat from working conditions research, partly because legislation and the factories inspectorate covered these areas, but also because of the move towards the individual as the object of strategies of regulation.

SELECTION

Since the First World War, the use of psychometric tests in an attempt to fit the worker to the job has dominated industrial psychology (Hollway, 1992). While training workers in the use of new methods was a significant early part of industrial psychology's work, selecting applicants for the various types of machine-paced work became increasingly prominent. Selection was based on the use of psychological tests for the measurement of various job-related skills such as visual acuity and finger dexterity. In 1933 Rowntree's labour manager published an article which claimed that the new methods "proved to be right in approximately 95% of instances" and that "the misfits have been practically halved" (Northcott, 1933, p. 168). Selection appeared to take over from fatigue as the practice which could be claimed as uniting the interests of efficiency and welfare: by "fitting the man to the job", he or she would not only be more efficient but more contented and "reduce to an almost negligible number the cases in which work is felt to be monotonous" (J. S. Rowntree, 1923, p. 245). It was claimed that even the most monotonous of jobs were suitable to some individuals, namely "the lowest grade of worker" (ibid). Women's "nature" provided a justification for situating them in dead-end and monotonous jobs (B. S. Rowntree, 1979, p. 139).

The *New York Times* of 17 February 1922, announcing the new Psychological Corporation whose aim was described as "the application of psychology to business", claimed: "Some of the backers of the Psychological Corporation believe that it would be possible to increase by $70,000,000,000 the national wealth each year by properly fitting every man, women and child to the kind of work each could best perform" (New Psychological Corporation in the USA, 1922, p. 76). Psychometrics, with its unique cocktail of "scientific" measurement, mass regulation, and the claim of enhanced productivity for business and the nation, put industrial psychology on the map.

Where psychometrics provided the method, the psychology of individual differences supplied the theory, which derived from social Darwinism and eugenics (Burt, 1953; Rose, 1985). The psychology of individual differences was recognized as quite distinct from laboratory psychology, as can be seen from Münsterberg's claim that "a complete change can be traced in our science" (1913, p. 10) and Burt's assertion of a "new, advanced and separate branch" which he called "individual differences in mind" (1924, p. 67). Viteles, whose textbook on industrial psychology succeeded Münsterberg's as the classic American text in the 1930s, explained the new psychology as follows:

> Industrial psychology is interested in the individual – in his reactions to a specific situation. The growth of industrial psychology has been associated with the development of psychology interested not in general tendencies, but in problems of a single individual and in the nature and extent of the variation of his response from the reactions of other individuals. (Viteles, 1933, p. 29)

This new emphasis brought engineering psychology and personnel psychology into "active conflict":

> The program of applied experimental psychology is to modify treatments so as to obtain the highest average performance when all persons are treated alike – a search, that is, for "the one best way". The program of applied correlational psychology is to raise average performance by treating persons differently – different job assignments, different therapies, different disciplinary methods. The correlationist is utterly antagonistic to a doctrine of "the one best way".... The ideal of the engineering psychologist, I am told, is to simplify jobs so that every individual in the working population will be able to perform them satisfactorily, i.e. so that differentiation of treatment will be unnecessary. (Cronbach, 1957, p. 678)

In the 1950s, however, the engineering tradition of job design, beseiged by its connections with scientific management, linked up with the new motivation theorists to produce ideas and practices concerning job enlargement and job satisfaction (Hollway, 1991, chap. 6) and thus started a not-too-successful move away from deskilling of jobs (Davis, Canter & Hoffman 1955; Walker, 1950).

HUMAN RELATIONS

Between the 1930s and the 1960s human relations became the dominant paradigm within which the management of people in organizations was understood and its practices modified. In its most popular and well-established sense, human relations "is simply a catch-all term for describing the way in which the people who comprise an organization think about and deal with each other' (Gellerman, 1966, p. 1). More precisely, it refers to a social-psychological paradigm for understanding the individual at work and to recommendations for management practice which stem from this approach. It is no more the exclusive property of psychology than of sociology or management theory. The practice of planned change outside the financial and technical spheres has taken place predominantly according to human relations emphases, notably motivation, leadership, and interpersonal skills.

A series of famous studies were conducted at "Hawthorne", a site of the Western Electric Company in a Chicago suburb, in the second half of the 1920s. Describing the reasons for the transition from the early illumination studies, Mayo (1949) comments:

> The conditions of scientific experiment had apparently been fulfilled – experimental room, control room; changes introduced one at a time; all other conditions held steady. And the results were perplexing. (p. 61)

Experimenters measured the effect on the productivity of women workers of a great variety of changes in working conditions, including illumination and rest pauses. Productivity increased under all conditions, a result that was attributed to the improved social relations. The extent to which this experiment became synonymous with the Hawthorne studies is evident in the way that this phenomenon is called the "Hawthorne effect". In 1928, Mayo (from the Harvard Business School) visited the plant. Also in 1928, an internal Industrial Research Division was set up to develop a massive interviewing programme to find out what was on employees' minds (Hollway, 1991, pp. 79ff; Roethlisberger & Dickson, 1970). According to Roethlisberger, one of the Harvard research team, in 1928 a new era of personnel relations began: "It was the first real attempt to get human data and to forge human tools to get them. In that year a novel idea was born; dimly the experimenters perceived a new method of human control" (Roethlisberger, 1949, p. 16)

The counselling programme which developed from this research at the Hawthorne works continued until 1956. In 1931, observation began in the Bank Wiring Room (all men employees), where restriction of output was first formally documented and investigated. The formal involvement of the Harvard team ended in 1932. The counselling programme led to training programmes in interpersonal skills (Roethlisberger, 1954) for supervisors, thus initiating a practice that was to become the bread and butter of human relations psychology.

The Hawthorne studies combined two radical departures from previous industrial psychology. The first involved a shift from the psychophysiological approach to the worker to a socio-emotional one. The second was a change in method from an experimental one whose object was the body (or the inter-face between the body and the job), to one whose object was attitudes as the intervening variable between situation (working conditions) and response (output). As Roethlisberger describes the conclusions of one set of studies (in the Relay Assembly Test Room): "What all their experiments had dramatically and conclusively demonstrated was the importance of employee attitudes and sentiments" (1949, p. 15). According to Roethlisberger (1949) the important characteristic of sentiments was that "they cannot be modified by logic alone" (p. 31). He described the early experimenters at Hawthorne as

> Carrying around in their heads the notion of "economic man", a man primarily motivated by economic interest, whose logical capacities were being used in the service of this self-interest. Gradually and painfully the experimenters had been forced to abandon this conception of the worker and his behavior ... they found that the behavior of workers could not be understood apart from their feelings or sentiments. (p. 19)

Human relations not only made possible the production of different kinds of information for the first time in the workplace, but also had a powerful effect on the workers themselves. The Hawthorne interview programme discovered that a sympathetic interview technique not only could elicit new information that was valuable to management, but also could itself be instrumental in effecting a change in employees' attitudes. Human relations training was later to be based on this insight (Hollway, 1991, chaps 5 & 6).

Attitudes and sentiments became the central human relations problematic because they gave conceptual leverage to a problem of resistance to control by workers in large organizations. Commentators as far apart politically as Braverman (famed for his Marxist analysis of deskilling and the labour process) and Drucker (the popular management writer) are of the opinion that scientific management was not superseded but was built into the technology of the production line. Drucker (quoted by Braverman, 1974, p. 87) states that Taylorism "is no longer the property of a faction, since its fundamental teachings have become the bedrock of all work design". Braverman develops this by examining the role of management and related behavioural sciences once the technology is in place:

> Work itself is organized according to Taylorian principles, while personnel departments and academics have busied themselves with the selection, training, manipulation, pacification, and adjustment of "manpower" to suit the work processes so organized. Taylorism dominates the world of production; the practitioners of "human relations" and "industrial psychology" are the maintenance crew for the human machinery. (p. 87)

During the 1960s, full employment, strong trade unions, and an anti-authoritarian culture combined to maintain the centrality of motivation as management's way of viewing the problem of employee regulation (Hollway, 1991, chap. 7). In the 1980s and 1990s unemployment and the curtailment of trade union power meant that the problematic shifted away from motivation towards efficiency. Encouragement to self-regulation is still a central issue, but in practice is increasingly targeted towards a core – professional, managerial, and technical – workforce (Hollway, 1991, chap. 9). In the future, the difference between core and peripheral workers will probably be the basis for differences in regulatory practices: the use of psychometric testing to determine who gets a job and who does not and developmental methods including the use of selection tests, but also counselling and human relations-type training for a core workforce which would be expensive to replace and on whose commitment the organization depends. The way that work is structured in future will affect the relative dominance of problems concerning the individual at work. If "the days of the large employment organization are over" (Handy, 1984, p. 86), the problematic of motivation, based on the imperative to produce employee self-regulation, is likely to be modified or transformed.

CONCLUSION

Each regulation strategy associated with work psychology has used a different lens through which to view the individual: scientific management, human factors, selection, interpersonal skills training, work design, and leadership. They vary in their success and in the advantages that accrue to employees from their use. Among these there is little theoretical coherence, and even within each broad strategy there are differences. This is because they are not primarily the products of theorizing, but of changing regulative problems in a variety of workplaces. They do share one common feature, however, and this testifies to the power of work psychology: they all target the individual.

Work psychology's legitimacy hinges on its claim to be scientific and therefore neutral. The historical evidence demonstrates, however, that this very claim was part of a wider set of power relations which meant that work psychology has predominantly been produced from a vantage point of management's concerns with the regulation of individual employees. The extent to which this functions on behalf of employees is a question that can be answered only by looking at specific practices in specific locations. None the less, work psychology's utility to management hinges on its claim to be in the interests of both efficiency and welfare simultaneously.

FURTHER READING

Baritz, L. (1965). *Servants of power*. Middletown, CT: Wesleyan University Press.
Hollway, W. (1991). *Work psychology and organizational behaviour: Managing the individual at work*. London: Sage.
Münsterberg, H. (1913). *Psychology and industrial efficiency*. Boston, MA: Houghton Mifflin.
Roethlisberger, F. J., & Dickson, W. J. (1970). *Management and the worker*. Cambridge, MA: Harvard University Press (original work published in 1939).
Rose, M. (1975). *Industrial behaviour: Theoretical development since Taylor*. Harmondsworth: Penguin.

REFERENCES

Baritz, L. (1965). *Servants of power*. Middletown, CT: Wesleyan University Press.
Birkbeck College (1961). *Birkbeck College Calendar*. London: Birkbeck College.
Braverman, H. (1974). *Labour and monopoly capital: The degradation of work in the twentieth century*. New York: Monthly Review Press.
Burt, C. (1924). The mental differences between individuals. *Journal of the National Institute of Industrial Psychology 11*(2), 67–74.
Burt, C. (1953). *Contribution of psychology to social problems*. London: Oxford University Press (originally L. T. Hobhouse memorial lecture no. 22).
Cadbury, E. (1914). Some principles of industrial organization: The case for and against scientific management. *Sociological Review*, 7(2), 99–117.
Chandler, A. D. (1977). *The visible hand: the managerial revolution in American business*. Cambridge, MA: Harvard University Press.
Cronbach, L. (1957). The two disciplines of scientific psychology. *American Psychologist*, 12, 671–684.
Davis, L., Canter, R., & Hoffman, J. (1955). Current job design criteria. *Journal of Industrial Engineering*, 6(2), 21–33.
Devinat, P. (1927). *Scientific management in Europe*. Geneva: International Labour Organization.

Farmer, E., & Eyre, A. B. (1922). An investigation into the packing of chocolates (1). *Journal of the National Institute of Industrial Psychology*, *1*(2), 14–16.

Gellerman, S. W. (1966). *The management of human relations*. Chicago, IL: Holt, Rinehart & Winston.

Goldman, P., & Van Houten, D. R. (1979). Bureaucracy and domination: Managerial strategy in turn-of-the-century American industry. In D. Dunkerley & G. Salaman (Eds) *International yearbook of organisation studies* (pp. 108–141). London: Routledge & Kegan Paul.

Handy, C. (1984). *The future of work*. Oxford: Basil Blackwell.

Hearnshaw, L., & Winterbourn, R. (1945). *Human welfare and industrial efficiency*. Wellington, NZ: Reed.

Herzberg, F. (1968). One more time: How do you motivate employees? *Harvard Business Review*, *46*, 53–62.

Herzberg, F., Mausner, B., & Snyderman, B. (1959). *The motivation to work*. New York: Wiley.

Hollway, W. (1991). *Work psychology and organizational behaviour: Managing the individual at work*. London: Sage.

Hollway, W. (1992). Occupational psychology and the regulation of work: The case of vocational selection. *Occupational Psychologist*, *16*, 2–9.

Hollway, W. (1993). Efficiency and welfare: Industrial psychology at Rowntree's cocoa works. *Theory and Psychology*, *3*.

Hoxie, R. F. (1915). *Scientific management and labor*. New York: Appleton.

McClelland, D. (1961). *The achieving society*. New York: Van Nostrand.

Mansion House meeting (1922). *Journal of the National Institute of Industrial Psychology*, *1*(2), 59–61.

Mayo, E. (1949). *The social problems of an industrial civilization*. London: Routledge & Kegan Paul.

Münsterberg, H. (1913). *Psychology and industrial efficiency*. Boston, MA: Houghton Mifflin.

Myers, C. S. (1926). *Industrial psychology in Great Britain*. London: Cape.

New Psychological Corporation in the USA (1922). *Journal of the National Institute of Industrial Psychology*, *1*, 76–78.

Northcott, C. H. (1933) Industrial psychology at Rowntree's cocoa works. (2) Statistical note upon the results of vocational selection, 1923–1931. *The Human Factor*, 166–168.

Occupational Psychology Section and Division joint meeting (1990). *The Psychologist*, *3*(8), 375.

Rodger, A. (1972). *Training and development* (unpublished course notes of Birkbeck College, Department of Occupational Psychology).

Roethlisberger, F. J. (1949). *Management and morale*. Cambridge, MA: Harvard University Press.

Roethlisberger, F. J. (1954). *Training for human relations*. Cambridge, MA: Harvard University Press.

Roethlisberger, F. J., & Dickson, W. J. (1970). *Management and the worker*. Cambridge, MA: Harvard University Press (original work published in 1939).

Rose, N. (1985) *The psychological complex: Psychology, politics and society in England, 1869–1939*. London: Routledge & Kegan Paul.

Rowntree, B. S. (1979). *The human factor in business*. New York: Arno Press (original work published 1921).

Rowntree, J. S. (1923). The scope of vocational selection in industry. *Journal of the National Institute of Industrial Psychology*, *1*(6), 240–245.

Shackel, B. (Ed.) (1974). *Applied ergonomics*. Guildford: IPC Science and Technology Press.

Shimmin, S. (1986). *History and natural history in occupational psychology* (keynote address to the BPS Occupational Psychology conference, University of Nottingham).

Shimmin, S., & Wallis, D. (1989). *Change and survival in occupational psychology*. Paper presented at the 4th West European Congress on The Psychology of Work and Organisation, Cambridge, 10–12 April.

"Some principles of industrial organization: The case for and against scientific management" (1914). *Sociological Review*, 7(2), 99–117.

Taylor, F. W. (1967). *The principles of scientific management*. New York: Norton (original work published 1911).

Viteles, M. S. (1933). *Industrial psychology*. London: Cape.

Walker, C. R. (1950). The problem of the repetitive job. *Harvard Business Review*, *58*(3), 54–58.

4

FORENSIC (CRIMINOLOGICAL) PSYCHOLOGY

Clive R. Hollin

University of Birmingham, England

The application of psychology to the fields of law and criminal behaviour has become one of the growth areas of applied psychology since the early 1980s. Research has flourished, for example, in such diverse areas as crime detection, exemplified by offender profiling; police selection and training; courtroom dynamics, including the impact of expert psychological evidence and legal decision-making (in both civil and criminal courts); rules of law in

53

mental health and juvenile and family legislation; the study of offenders, as with sex offenders and juvenile delinquents; and the design and impact of crime prevention programmes. While there is a fine line to be drawn in much of this research between criminology, sociology, psychiatry, and psychology, there are several texts that offer an overview of psychology, law, and criminal behaviour from a psychological perspective (Hollin, 1989, 1992; Kagehiro & Laufer, 1992; Lloyd-Bostock, 1988; Quay, 1987; Raskin, 1989).

While driven by theory and empirical research, forensic psychology is very much an applied field. Forensic psychologists work in many different settings, including prisons, courts, hospitals and other treatment facilities, probation services, police services, and government departments. They tackle a vast array of work, spanning consultancy, training, research, management, treatment, and giving expert evidence in court. Clearly it is not possible to cover all these topics in one chapter. Therefore I shall concentrate here on three areas that exemplify the range and scope of both theory and practice in contemporary forensic psychology – psychology in the courtroom, advances in theories of criminal behaviour, and impact of these theories on crime prevention strategies.

PSYCHOLOGY IN THE COURTROOM

The idea that psychology might have something to offer in the courtroom is not a new one. As long ago as 1908 Hugo Münsterberg suggested that psychology could usefully be applied to the study of eyewitness evidence and to the dynamics of the jury, while the psychologist would have much to offer in the role of an expert witness. Münsterberg's choice of topics for psychological research has stood the test of time, although as Diamond (1992) remarks, "Vigorous and sustained research in the field is a recent phenomenon. It is only 15 years since the first review of psychology and law appeared in the *Annual Review of Psychology*" (p. v).

Many forensic psychology practitioners will appear in the courtroom. The discussion below on the topic of evidence illustrates the theoretical, professional, and applied issues that face psychologists engaged in this type of work.

Eyewitness evidence

With a relatively long history, the psychological study of eyewitness memory provides an excellent illustration of the methods and controversies in legal psychology. It is not difficult to see why psychologists turned to the study of eyewitness memory, involving as it does the psychological processes of perception and memory, together with the opportunity to address a major concern of all those working in the justice system – the possibility of a wrongful conviction. Indeed, Huff and Rattner (1988) have suggested that "the single most important factor contributing to wrongful conviction is eyewitness misidentification" (p. 135).

The study of eyewitness evidence has generated a vast body of research collected in a number of books (e.g., Lloyd-Bostock & Clifford, 1983; Wells & Loftus, 1984), and discussed in several review articles (e.g., Goodman & Hahn, 1987; Williams, Loftus, & Deffenbacher, 1992). The force of this research has been to show how a range of variables can influence eyewitness memory and hence eyewitness evidence. These variables are generally referred to in the context of the three stages of *acquisition*, *retention* (or *storage*), and *retrieval* traditionally delineated in memory research. Through laboratory research it has become clear that memory for real-life events can be significantly affected at all three stages. Thus, variables operative at the stage of acquisition, such as the length of time spent in observation and the level of violence, can influence the accuracy of eyewitness recall and recognition. Storage variables, such as the length of time between viewing and recollection and talking with other witnesses can similarly influence eyewitness testimony. Finally, the same is true for retrieval factors as exemplified by the style of questioning used to elicit testimony and the impact of misleading information. In addition, individual differences such as the age of the witness may play a role across all three stages.

While much of the early research pointed to the somewhat fragile nature of eyewitness evidence, this knowledge base proved to be the foundation for a further research effort with the practical goal of enhancing eyewitness evidence. A body of psychological research has developed around, for example, the design and use of face recall systems such as the photofit and identikit procedures (Davies, 1983); the fairness of the identity parade or line-up (Cutler & Penrod, 1988); artist sketches (Davies, 1986); and improved interview techniques such as the cognitive interview (Fisher, Geiselman, & Amador, 1989).

The law–psychology debate

The psychological study of eyewitness evidence has generated debate in three areas. The first hinges on the theoretical interpretation of the findings from the research into leading questions. Specifically, there is a view that misleading information actually changes memory, so that recall of the original event is impossible (Loftus & Ketcham, 1983). Alternatively, other theorists hold that the misleading information coexists with the original memory and can be accessed given the right retrieval cues (Zaragoza, McCloskey, & Jarvis, 1987). These different positions and the experimental studies they generate clearly add to the richness of theoretical discussion within cognitive psychology.

The second area of debate centres on the generalizability of the experimental evidence, that is, the degree to which findings from mainly laboratory-based studies can be applied to "real-world" issues. Two studies have found high levels of similarity between eyewitness performance in laboratory and real-world settings (Brigham, Maass, Snyder, & Spaulding, 1982; Sanders & Warnick, 1981). Yuille and Cutshall (1986) found, however, that eyewitnesses to a real-life incident did not perform in a manner consistent with the research literature. This is an area in which further empirical studies are needed, gathering data from an amalgam of methodologies including laboratory studies, case-studies, field-studies, and study of archival sources.

The third area of debate, flowing from the second, concerns the presentation in court by forensic psychologists of the research findings, neatly including Münsterberg's role for the psychologist as an expert witness. The argued lack of generalizability of the findings is said by critics to restrict their usefulness generally, and may act to increase juror scepticism resulting in wrong verdicts being reached. In addition, the suggestion has also been advanced that jurors have an intuitive, commonsense appreciation of human behaviour that will allow them to judge when an eyewitness is likely to be inaccurate. The nature of the results from psychological research has also been a cause for debate. The experimental studies on which the forensic psychologist draws typically produce findings based on probabilities rather than statements of what is certainly true or false or right and wrong. Thus psychological research cannot predict whether a given eyewitness is correct or incorrect in, say, his or her identification of a suspect. Williams, Loftus, & Deffenbacher (1992) discuss these objections and conclude that confidence can be held in the reliability of the research findings; that expert testimony is needed to inform lay understanding of eyewitness testimony but that this does not adversely affect juror scepticism; and that probabilistic statements do not necessarily conflict with the role of the expert witness. In the final analysis the issue facing the forensic psychologist is one of individual ethical and moral judgement: potential expert witnesses must consider their belief in the strength of the evidence then, as Wells (1986) notes, "consider the potential effects of not giving expert testimony" (p. 83).

Confession evidence

Whatever the finer points of debate concerning the research evidence, it is undeniable that psychologists have brought the complexity of the issue of eyewitness evidence squarely into the public domain. The same is also true of another form of evidence – confessional evidence. As was once the case with eyewitness evidence, confessional evidence is accorded a great deal of weight in reaching decisions of guilt and innocence. If a person confesses to a crime, then this counts significantly towards a guilty verdict. However, a number of cases in England in the early 1990s, including the Guildford Four and the Birmingham Six, have shaken the public's faith in a criminal justice system that places such high value on uncorroborated confessional evidence. As with eyewitness evidence, forensic psychologists have been in a position to offer the courts both empirical evidence and a coherent explanation for the phenomenon of false confessions (Gudjonsson, 1992).

Kassin and Wrightsman (1985) outlined three types of false confession: first, the *voluntary confession* offered in the absence of any external pressure; second, the *coerced-compliant confession* made during police interrogation and which the confessor knows to be false; and third, the *coerced-internalized confession* in which during interrogation confessors come wrongly to believe, either temporarily or permanently, that they committed the crime of which they are accused. While voluntary confessions may be a sign of psychological distress, it is the latter two types of confessions that have attracted most attention from researchers.

The research into confessions has focused on the conditions under which the interrogation takes place, the tactics of police interrogation, and the psychological characteristics of the individual likely to make a false confession. In terms of conditions, it is plain that the experience of police custody can be stressful, placing the suspect in a vulnerable position. With regard to interrogational tactics, the police have developed sophisticated questioning techniques designed to exert maximum pressure on the suspect to confess (e.g., Inbau, Reid, & Buckley, 1986). Gudjonsson and Clark (1986) suggested that in seeking to cope with the demands of stress and interrogation, some individuals will be coerced into making false confessions. The *compliant* suspect, who knowingly gives a false confession, is characterized by generally low intelligence, high acquiescence (i.e., a tendency to answer questions in the affirmative), and a high need for social approval. *Suggestible* suspects, however, internalize the interrogator's messages and come to believe that they committed the crime, leading to false confessions. A summary of the experimental findings, reviewed by Gudjonsson (1992), describing the characteristics of the suggestible individual is shown in Table 1.

Psychological research has contributed significantly to the legal debate on the standing of uncorroborated confessions. It will doubtless be the case that the same issues detailed above in the law–psychology debate regarding eyewitness evidence will again be rehearsed for confessions. None the less, to be debating the issues from a psychological perspective is rapid progress, given the recent nature of much of the empirical work.

The jury

As Hans (1992) notes, while jury trials are decreasing in frequency, the jury continues to attract a great deal of research. Alongside the intricacy of the psychological processes involved, the jury continues to interest researchers, Hans suggests, because jury trials are often of social and political significance, including a critical role in death penalty cases in most US states.

Table 1 Psychological correlates of suggestibility

Psychological factor	Relationship with suggestibility
Acquiescence	Positive
Anxiety	Positive
Assertiveness	Negative
Facilitative coping style	Negative
Fear of negative evaluation	Positive
High expectation of accuracy	Positive
Intelligence	Negative
Memory ability	Negative
Self-esteem	Negative
Social desirability	Positive

Note: A positive relationship predicts that, say, as anxiety increases so suggestibility also increases; a negative relationship predicts, say, that as assertiveness increases suggestibility decreases.

The concerns of psychologists have been mainly in the four areas of jury selection and composition, extra-evidential influences, the impact of evidence, and decision-making.

Jury selection and composition

There are criteria, such as age and eligibility to vote, that inform the selection of individuals to sit on juries. However, the issue runs rather deeper than these formal criteria, in that an ideal juror would have sufficient intelligence to comprehend the evidence; would have the verbal and social skills to contribute to jury discussion prior to reaching a verdict; and would be unbiased and non-prejudicial at all times. In the real world, unfortunately, the ideal juror is a rare commodity: a number of studies have shown that juror verdicts can be heavily influenced by the age, sex, and psychological attributes of the jurors. For example, some people place undue faith in the state and the prosecution, believing that mistakes in the criminal justice system are infrequent. Clearly, it would not be in the best interests of justice to have a jury stacked with such individuals, and therefore some means of selection for jury service is needed. In the USA particularly psychologists have made their voice heard in the debate over the utility of "scientific jury selection". This approach to selection utilizes techniques such as polling public opinion to gauge normative attitudes and hence to profile ideal jurors; analysis of mock juror debates to inform selection and presentation of evidence; and assessment of jurors before the trial begins to identify "unsuitable" candidates. This procedure has generated considerable controversy, both in terms of the ethics of selection and the validity of the techniques themselves.

58

Extra-evidential influences

While one might hope that juror decision-making would be entirely based on the evidence presented in court, there are fears that extra-evidential factors may influence jurors. There are three likely sources of extra-evidential influence: pre-trial publicity, witness confidence, and the juror's perceptions and attitudes towards others in the courtroom.

Looking first at pretrial publicity, the typical experimental strategy is to give groups of mock jurors newspaper cuttings about a defendant in which details of previous criminal history, retracted confession, and so on are varied. In their overview of this research, Linz and Penrod (1992) drew the conclusion that "information about prior convictions and confessions may indeed be detrimental to criminal defendants. Emotional, sensational, or gruesome descriptions of the crime may also have an impact on juror decision making" (p. 11). Of course, judges can instruct jurors to disregard pre-trial publicity, but do such instructions translate into action? From the limited experimental evidence, the answer is in the negative. Judges' instructions appear to do little to eliminate the biasing influence of pre-trial publicity.

With regard to the impact of witness confidence, the weight of evidence from mock juror studies strongly suggests that jurors are more likely to return a guilty verdict after hearing evidence from a confident witness. Similarly, less credibility is accorded to the evidence from a hesitant, uncertain witness (Penrod & Cutler, 1987). Now, if confidence is a reliable index of accuracy, then this is not a matter for undue concern. On the other hand, if there is a grain of truth in Ambrose Bierce's observation that to be positive is to be wrong at the top of one's voice, then clearly this introduces a source of extra-evidential influence. The findings from studies of the relationship between confidence and accuracy bear witness to the truth of Bierce's witticism: at best confidence is arguably but a weak predictor of witness accuracy.

Finally, can jurors' perceptions, attitudes, and judgements be swayed by interpersonal factors rather than the evidence? In their overview of the research, Hans and Vidmar (1986) identified a range of such potential influences: for example, the physical attractiveness of the defendant can lead to a favourable outcome for the defendant (although more attractive defendants who offered little justification for their actions were seen as deserving a *more* severe sentence); defendants with high socio-economic status were seen as less blameworthy for their crime; and women are less likely than men to be found guilty for reasons of insanity. Other subtle influences on jurors include "powerful speech" (speaking clearly and without hesitation) by witnesses and defendants; the age of the witness; and the defendant's demeanour in court.

Strengths and weaknesses

Any field of applied psychology is bound to meet its critics who dismiss its theories, its methods, its appreciation of real world issues, and the generalizability of the evidence it produces. It would be naïve in the extreme to deny that there are strengths and weaknesses in studies in forensic psychology. Mock jury studies, for example, are easy meat for critics: they are removed from the drama of the courtroom, they do not always use trial procedures, they concentrate unduly on one variable, they rely heavily on undergraduate participants, and so on. However, rather than dismissing the research findings as worthless, as do some critics, it is more constructive to acknowledge the limitations of the studies and to seek to improve and broaden research methods. In that way weak findings can be identified and robust findings presented with greater certainty. Indeed, cases in which findings from social psychology were used to set legal precedence (Colman, 1991) should motivate researchers to seek ways to strengthen their procedures so that their findings can have an even greater impact on legal proceedings.

THEORIES OF CRIMINAL BEHAVIOUR

The search for an explanation for criminal behaviour has a long history, with distinguished contributions from many disciplines including psychology. As mainstream psychological theories rise to favour, so they have been applied to the phenomenon of criminal behaviour: for example, there have been psychoanalytic and psychodynamic theories, personality theories, constitutional theories, and learning theories (Hollin, 1989). While these theories all have their modern-day advocates, the current trends in psychological theorizing lie in the application of social learning theory and cognitive theory to formulate explanations of criminal behaviour. As will be seen, after a discussion of the theory, these theoretical advances have had a significant practical impact on crime prevention.

Social learning theory

The emergence of a social learning approach to the explanation of criminal behaviour can be traced to a line of theorizing, beginning with Sutherland's (1939) *differential association theory*, that emphasized the importance of learning in understanding criminal behaviour. Briefly, Sutherland took the view that crime itself is defined by those people within society with the power to make laws. Once defined, there are some people who abide by the rules and others who transgress. Why this difference in law-abiding behaviour? The answer, Sutherland proposed, is to be found in learning – learning that is no different in nature from any other human learning. Through association with individuals disposed to break the law, some people acquire not only the specific skills to commit offences but also the attitudes and motivations that favour breaking the law. In total, differential association theory incorporates three fundamental psychological assumptions: first, the crucial learning takes place within close social groups; second, the learning has both a cognitive and a performance component; and third, criminal behaviour is acquired behaviour and not a sign of deep-seated psychopathology. While all three assumptions would meet with sympathy from contemporary psychologists, at the time Sutherland was writing the basic theoretical structures to explain learning were not well advanced.

In seeking to offer an account of the process of learning, Jeffery (1965) suggested that operant theory could be used to refine differential association theory, giving *differential reinforcement theory*. In essence, Jeffery proposed that criminal behaviour is an operant behaviour: in other words, criminal behaviour is acquired and maintained by the reinforcing and punishing consequences it produces for the individual concerned. For example, in most cases of acquisitive criminal behaviour, such as theft and burglary, the consequences are financial gain. In turn, these gains make it more likely that the behaviour will be repeated when the occasion for a successful crime arises.

The advent of social learning theory (Bandura, 1977), in part an extension of operant principles, heralded the next theoretical step. Social learning theory departs from operant theory in the way it explains the acquisition of behaviour and the forces that maintain behaviour. In operant theory the acquisition of behaviour is through direct environmental reinforcement, in social learning theory the process of acquisition is extended to include modelling and imitation. The specific models for criminal behaviour are to be found in the social environment: in the actions of family and peers, in the prevalent sub-culture, and in cultural symbols as found on television and in magazines. The maintenance of criminal behaviour is, as in operant theory, not only via external reinforcement such as financial and social gain, but also through *internal* rewards such as increased self-esteem and self-reinforcing thoughts and through the nature of the appraisals of one's actions. These self-appraisals or *definitions* may be positive, in that the criminal behaviour is seen as desirable: for example, football hooligans may define their actions as exciting. Alternatively, the definitions may be neutralizing, serving to justify the criminal behaviour: for example, people who falsify their tax returns may say that the sums are so small that they do not matter, or that as there is no real victim so no harm is done as with "real" crimes. These definitions, clearly demanding complex cognitive processes, serve to set the meaning of their behaviour for the individuals concerned. As Akers (1990) suggests, social learning theory offers perhaps the most psychologically complete theory of criminal behaviour. One of the impacts of social learning theory, and of the cognitive revolution generally in mainstream psychology, has been to turn researchers' attention to the nature and role of cognition.

In the study of criminal behaviour, this trend has been manifest in studies of social cognition both in terms of cognitive style and cognitive processing.

Cognition and crime: cognitive style

In their review of cognition and crime, Ross and Fabiano (1985) make the distinction between *im*personal cognition and *inter*personal (i.e., social) cognition. The former is concerned with our knowledge of our physical world, the latter with our attitudes and beliefs about our social world. Various styles of social cognition have been associated with criminal behaviour, particularly juvenile delinquency, as outlined below. It should be noted, however, that these are trends in the literature: it is not the case that every study reaches the same conclusion, findings can vary for reasons such as sampling and design. Further, it should not be assumed that every offender will display these cognitive styles: these are general trends in offender populations *not* the defining characteristics of all offenders.

Empathy

The ability to see the world, including one's own behaviour, from another person's point of view is to display empathy. A number of studies have suggested that offender populations do not score highly on measures of empathy.

Locus of control

The concept of locus of control refers to the degree to which individuals perceive their behaviour to be under their own *internal* control, as opposed to being under the control of *external* forces such as luck or authority. The general empirical trend is that offenders see themselves as externally controlled. However, this may vary with the type of offence: violent young offenders, for example, show greater external control than non-violent young offenders (Hollin & Wheeler, 1982).

Moral reasoning

The broad conclusion across studies is that delinquency is associated with a delay in the development of moral reasoning (Nelson, Smith, & Dodd, 1990). However, as with locus of control, this may be tempered by type of offence. Thornton and Reid (1982) found that young offenders who had committed offences without financial gain, such as assault, murder, and sex offences, displayed more mature moral judgement than offenders convicted for crimes of acquisition such as burglary and theft.

Self-control

A lack of self-control is often associated with impulsive behaviour: a failure to stop and think between impulse and action. It is a finding of long standing in psychological research that offender populations are characterized by low levels of self-control (and hence high levels of impulsivity).

Knowledge of these styles of social cognition offers a general impression of the way that some offenders may view their social world. However, to achieve a more rounded picture, these "fixed" styles should be set in the more dynamic context of social information processing.

Cognition and crime: social information processing

The impact of theories of social information processing have been most keenly felt in the study of aggressive and violent behaviour. Dodge (1986) defined a sequence of steps in the effective cognitive processing of social information leading up to a given action: (1) the encoding of social cues; (2) the cognitive representation and interpretation of these social cues; (3) searching for the appropriate ways to respond in a given situation; (4) deciding on the optimum response.

The first part of this cognitive sequence involves the individual in perceiving and interpreting situational cues, especially the words and actions of other people. There is a body of research evidence that strongly suggests that aggressive and violent people, perhaps particularly aggressive and violent children and adolescents, search for and perceive *fewer* social cues than non-violent people. Yet further, it is likely that violent individuals will interpret the behaviour of others in a hostile manner (Slaby & Guerra, 1988). Indeed, this hostile aggressive interpretation of the actions of other people may well be a fundamental component of violent behaviour.

The next part of the sequence, following one's understanding of the situation, involves the generation of suitable responses for that situation. This particular cognitive ability is referred to as *social problem solving*. A number of studies with both male and female young offenders have shown that, compared to non-delinquents, offenders used a more limited range of alternatives to solve interpersonal problems, and in selecting a response rely more on verbal and physical aggression (Freedman, Rosenthal, Donahue, Schlundt, & McFall, 1978). It also appears that in many instances the violent response is seen as legitimate and acceptable. Yet further, it is now generally accepted that emotional arousal can have a complex interaction with angry cognition, intensifying the person's aggression and increasing the likelihood of a violent outburst (Novaco & Welsh, 1989).

There are two competing explanations for the finding of limited social problem solving in offenders. The first is in terms of a "cognitive skills deficit", in that for whatever reason some offenders have not mastered the

63

skills necessary to generate a range of alternative solutions to cope with social problems. The second explanation focuses on the offender *defining* a given interaction as aggressive or hostile. Once this meaning is ascribed to a situation, albeit on the basis of limited utilization of social information, then it may well be the case that violent situations simply offer less alternatives for action. Following this line of thought, the decision to act in a violent manner becomes more reasonable: if you perceive that you are being threatened, then to decide to retaliate in kind is a defensible, even rational and legitimate, response.

These two interpretations of the research highlight a debate that has been running for centuries and has once again come to the forefront in contemporary exchanges (Roshier, 1989). With a "deficit" approach the antisocial behaviour is explained in terms of a failure to acquire cognitive skills and hence control over one's actions. Thus the individual's disposition to act in a criminal manner is seen as being determined by interactions between psychological, biological, social, and cultural forces. Alternatively, one might follow the rational "free choice" position, in which it is held that the person could equally as well have decided not to behave in a criminal manner as to elect to commit an offence.

Disposition or rational choice?

While dispositional theories of criminal behaviour were popular among many human scientists in the first decades of the twentieth century, during the 1970s there was a growing disenchantment with this approach to understanding criminal behaviour. Around this time a new approach began to emerge that saw human actions not as the product of social or psychological dispositions, but as the product of rational decisions motivated simply by self-interest and the expected gain to be had from the criminal behaviour. According to this latter view, there are two necessary events that must coincide for a crime to take place. First, there must be the opportunity for the crime; second, the individual must freely decide that the potential gains to be had from seizing the opportunity outweigh the potential losses if apprehended. A body of research evidence has, indeed, shown that many forms of criminal behaviour are related to increased opportunity and that offenders do make rational choices when faced with the opportunity to commit a crime (Cornish & Clarke, 1986). Now, while the conflict between dispositional and rational choice approaches raises several obvious philosophical and theoretical points, it also has an applied element in terms of crime prevention.

CRIME PREVENTION

There is nothing so useful as a good theory, and there are two crime prevention strategies in which the theoretical advances noted above have played a prominent role. The first strategy attempts to change the environment in which crime takes place; the second strategy seeks to change the person who commits the crime. The former approach has become known as *situational crime prevention*, the latter as *offender rehabilitation*.

Situational crime prevention

If we take the view that criminal behaviour stems from the opportunity to commit a crime in the knowledge that the potential gains outweigh the penalties, then it follows that in order to prevent crime we must reduce opportunity and/or increase the risk of detection. Such an approach holds, therefore, that crime prevention should focus on changing the situations in which crime takes place, rather than attempting to change the person after the crime has been committed. This approach to crime prevention has attracted the attention not only of researchers (e.g., Heal & Laycock, 1986), but also of politicians. As will be seen, many of the initiatives that have sprung from this political (and financial) investment have become part of our everyday lives.

Reducing opportunity

One way to reduce the opportunity for crime is known as *target hardening*: in practice this means physically strengthening the target or using security devices. The British Telecommunications company, for example, adopted this strategy by replacing aluminium coin boxes with steel boxes in seeking, with some degree of success, to reduce theft from telephone kiosks. Similarly, car damage and theft can be discouraged by the use of stronger and more sophisticated door locks, lockable wheel nuts, security coded sound systems, and car alarms. *Target removal* is another strategy aimed at reducing opportunity: payment of wages by direct bank credit, for example, removes the target of large amounts of cash being transported in public.

Increasing the risk of detection

One of the most obvious ways to increase the risk of detection is to increase levels of *formal surveillance*, particularly in situations where there is an increased likelihood of crime. While a police officer on every street corner would probably cut down crime significantly, this would have costs in terms of money and civil liberties. However, it does make sense for the police force to be present in increased numbers at sporting events such as football matches, and to patrol video and amusement arcades where truants from school (a high crime group) may congregate during school hours.

Alongside a human presence, such as a police officer, shop assistant, or car park attendant, technological advances have increased the potential for formal surveillance. Since closed-circuit television (CCTV) was used to cut down crime on the London Underground (Burrows, 1980), it has become widely used in banks, shops, and at sporting events. CCTV can, in theory, both deter and help to apprehend offenders. One of the most recent technological advances lies in the procedure known as *electronic monitoring* or *tagging*. Tagging involves convicted offenders wearing a small transmitter on their bodies, usually on the arm, ankle, or wrist. In one system the offenders are required to log in to a central computer via a telephone link in their homes: failure to log in would alert monitoring officers who are sent to investigate. Another system allows for constant monitoring via a device attached to the telephone system that picks up the transmitter's signals and relays them to a computer. If the offender moves out of a predetermined range from the telephone, say 30 metres, the monitoring officers are alerted. As noted by both British (e.g., Nellis, 1991) and US sources (e.g., Maxfield & Baumer, 1990), tagging has increased greatly in use since the mid-1980s.

Given the high cost of formal surveillance, strategies designed to increase *informal surveillance* have also been developed during the 1980s. Of the various strategies, there can be little doubt that Neighbourhood Watch (sometimes called Block Watch) has proved the most pervasive. Watch schemes have proliferated in North America (Brantingham & Brantingham, 1990), while Mayhew, Elliott, and Dowds (1989) estimate that in excess of 2.5 million households in England and Wales are Watch members. The principle underlying Watch schemes is simple: with the support of the police, people living close to one another take responsibility for the surveillance of each others' property, look out for suspicious characters, and report any signs of suspicious activity to the police. Indeed, the co-operation between police and public is a corner-stone of the scheme, encapsulated in the much-vaunted slogan "Crime: Together We'll Crack It".

Do Watch schemes work? In truth, the evidence is mixed, depending greatly on the operational definition of "work". Brantingham and Brantingham (1990) offer a concise statement: "The weight of evidence accumulated through evaluation studies conducted in North America and Britain now suggest that Watch programs may substantially improve participants' general attitudes about their neighbourhoods and may reduce participants' fear levels, but may not have much impact on crime" (p. 24).

There are other strategies, such as the design of streets and buildings, and the development of personal skills and strategies to avoid crime-prone settings, employed in situational crime prevention. However, there are complications to situational approaches to crime prevention that revolve around displacement and civil liberty.

Displacement

Do situational crime prevention strategies stop crime, or do they simply move it to another setting, time, or victim? It is clear that displacement can occur:

the evaluation of the introduction of CCTV on the London Underground hinted that crime had been displaced to those stations without CCTV close by those with the increased surveillance. Unfortunately, one of the major problems when attempting to establish whether an initiative has caused displacement on a large scale lies in untangling the crime statistics. Changes in the number of recorded crimes can be caused by many factors, making the influence of displacement effects, if any, extremely difficult to estimate. However, all things considered, it is unlikely that the human element can be discounted. It is plausible that some "occasional offenders" will be deterred by situational measures, while "professional offenders" will displace their criminal activity.

Civil liberties

Given that they change our environment, situational crime prevention measures raise questions about the society in which we live. A one level there are personal issues such as being recorded on videotape in banks and stores, carrying a personal identification card, and so on. At another level there are the implications of initiatives such as tagging: do we want a criminal justice system that uses electronic monitoring of fellow citizens? As discussed by Nellis (1991), technological advances may well make it feasible to implant transmitters under the skin so that in conjunction with CCTV the system could be used to monitor and hence control an individual's movements with hitherto undreamed-of precision. It is clear that society has some hard decisions to make regarding the balance between tolerance of crime and preservation of existing freedoms.

Offender rehabilitation

In 1974 Robert Martinson published a paper entitled "What works? Questions and answers about prison reform". The message that this paper delivered was that when it comes to the rehabilitation of offenders, "nothing works". This doctrine of "nothing works" has, in the time since Martinson's paper, become an article of faith, accepted by both academics and policy-makers alike. It is interesting to speculate as to why the "nothing works" doctrine found such ready acceptance.

If we follow the reasoning of researchers such as Andrews (e.g., Andrews, 1990; Andrews et al., 1990), then we see that the idea of rehabilitation must have a large psychological component. To design and conduct effective rehabilitation programmes, some sophistication in the skills needed to work with individual offenders is a necessity. This focus on the individual is clearly an area in which psychologists might claim some expertise. Yet, the concept of rehabilitation implicitly contains the assumption, with all the associated theoretical connotations, that criminal behaviour can be changed by working with the offender. As Andrews suggests, this focus on the individual offender – in both a practical and theoretical sense – runs counter to the sociological and political dominance evident in some mainstream criminology. The concept of rehabilitation, with its emphasis on understanding and working with the individual offender, stands in stark contrast to theories of crime that emphasize, for example, the role of a capitalist economy in creating crime. It follows that such theories see not rehabilitation but political change as the means by which to reduce crime. Thus the "nothing works" position is entirely suited to those theorists who espoused theories of crime that paid little attention to the offender and were hence opposed to the need for any psychologically oriented account of criminal behaviour. However, as West (1980) points out, the goals of social reform and individual change do not have to be exclusive.

At a political level the view that nothing works in offender rehabilitation received a favourable reception in the political climate of the 1970s and 1980s. The marked political swings to the right in the USA, the UK, and parts of continental Europe brought about changes in the criminal justice system based not on the soft liberal ideal of rehabilitation, but on policies steeped in the hard conservative neo-classical assertions of the need for deterrence and justice through punishment. Thus, as Cullen and Gendreau (1989) note, the "nothing works" doctrine perfectly suited the mood of the times, and was elevated from the status of theoretical argument to socially constructed reality. Against this academic and political backdrop the policies generated by a belief in the futility of rehabilitation were easy to implement – where, after all, was the opposition? Who was there to produce the evidence to state the case for effective rehabilitation? (Assuming, of course, that policies are based on reasoned empirical debate – which might be a very large assumption to make.)

In fairness there was always a voice of opposition with some writers – most notably Paul Gendreau and Robert Ross (e.g., Gendreau & Ross, 1979, 1987) – holding the line that effective rehabilitation was not an impossible goal and pointing to examples of success. However, a problem faced by these champions of rehabilitation lay in making a coherent case from a myriad of research findings. In the field of offender rehabilitation, reviewers are faced with many different types of interventions, conducted in different settings, with different measures of "success". As there are hundreds of outcome studies, it is very difficult, if not impossible, to draw meaningful conclusions about what works, for whom, and under what conditions, simply by pooling the results of several hundred studies and "vote counting". Indeed, as Gendreau and Andrews (1990) note, such an approach can lead to the neglect of key information, the formulation of imprecise conclusions, and even author bias. However, the development of the statistical technique of *meta-analysis* has gone some way towards providing a means by which to produce a standardized overview of many empirical studies.

A brief summary of the meta-analytic studies

As Izzo and Ross (1990) explain, meta-analysis is

a technique that enables a reviewer to objectively and statistically analyze the findings of each study as data points. . . . The procedure of meta-analysis involves collecting relevant studies, using the summary statistics from each study as a unit of analysis, and then analysing the aggregated data in a quantitative manner using statistical tests. (p. 135)

For example, in a typical meta-analytic study, Garrett (1985) included in her analysis 111 studies reported between 1960 and 1983, involving data gathered from a total of 13,055 young offenders. From this type of large-scale analysis, informed conclusions can be made about whether treatment works, and estimates made of what type of intervention works best in what setting.

When considering the findings of the meta-analytic studies, it is important to make a clear distinction between *clinical/personal and criminogenic* outcome variables. The former can be thought of as some dimension of personal functioning, such as psychological adjustment, cognition, anger control, skill level, and academic ability; while the latter refers specifically to variables concerned with crime, recidivism, type of offence, and so on. As a generalization, rehabilitation programmes with specific *clinical* aims tend to produce beneficial *clinical* outcomes regarding personal change. Thus, for example, programmes designed to improve social skills in offender populations do generally lead to positive changes in social competence (Hollin, 1990a). However, it is possible for programmes to produce significant outcomes in terms of positive personal change, but for that personal change to have no impact on *criminogenic* variables (Hollin, 1990b; Hollin & Henderson, 1984). One contribution of the meta-analytic studies is that they allow us to begin to untangle the confusion in the literature between these two types of outcome measure.

In the field of offender rehabilitation there have been several meta-analytic studies since Garret's 1985 publication; as with most research, later studies are able to build upon and avoid the criticisms levelled at earlier efforts. The discussion below is guided by the findings of two important meta-analytic studies (Andrews et al., 1990; Lipsey, 1992). In particular, the Lipsey study is a major piece of work, involving an analysis of 443 outcome studies in field of juvenile delinquency.

The first point to emerge from the meta-analyses is that there is a substantial variability of criminogenic outcome in the literature. As Lipsey notes, some studies show high effects of intervention on recidivism, in keeping perhaps with the position of writers such as Paul Gendreau and Robert Ross; while other studies show either no treatment effect or even a negative effect, in line with the views of the advocates of "nothing works". Given this variability it is understandable that different reviewers, depending on their sampling of the literature and their definitions of "success", have arrived at different conclusions.

What elements of a rehabilitation programme are associated with changes in offending? The meta-analysis studies allow an identification of the factors that characterize intervention programmes that show a high effect in *reducing criminal behaviour.*

First, indiscriminate targeting of treatment programmes is counterproductive in reducing recidivism: important predictors of success are that medium to high-risk offenders should be selected, and that programmes should focus on criminogenic areas. Second, the type of treatment programme is important: the structured and focused treatments, typically behavioural, skill-oriented, and multimodal programmes are more effective than less structured approaches such as counselling. Third, the most successful studies, while behavioural in nature, include a cognitive component to focus on the attitudes, values, and beliefs that offenders use to support and justify their antisocial behaviour. Fourth, regarding the type and style of service, Andrews et al. (1990) in particular suggest that some therapeutic approaches are not suitable for general use with offenders. Specifically, they argue that 'traditional psychodynamic and nondirective client-centered therapies are to be avoided within general samples of offenders' (p. 376). Fifth, treatment programmes conducted in the community have a stronger effect on delinquency than residential programmes. While residential programmes can be effective, they should be linked structurally with community-based interventions. Finally, the most effective programmes have high "treatment integrity" in that they are carried out by trained staff and the treatment initiators are involved in all the operational phases of the treatment programmes. In other words, there is effective management of a sound rehabilitation programme based on social learning and cognitive principles (Hollin, 1990b). Added to this list is the further conclusion made by Roberts and Camasso (1991), following their meta-analysis, that interventions specifically targeted at the family are also successful in reducing delinquency.

In total, given the above conditions, the meta-analysis studies suggest that the high-effect outcome studies can produce decreases in recidivism of the order of 20–40 per cent over and above the baseline levels from mainstream criminal sanctioning of offenders. On this basis it is fair to conclude that it is not the case that "nothing works" in attempts to rehabilitate offenders. Indeed, this point is reinforced by Thornton's (1987) searching re-examination of the studies cited by Martinson (1974); although Martinson (1979) had himself begun to withdraw from the "nothing works" position. It can be stated with confidence that rehabilitation programmes, particularly those based on the principles detailed above, can be effective in significantly reducing recidivism. Of course this conclusion has obvious benefits at every level: it offers the potential to reduce victimization; it takes the offender out of the criminal justice system, to the potential benefit of both individual offenders and their families; and it reduces the financial burden on taxpayers.

CONCLUSION

While this chapter has illustrated some of the topics in forensic psychology, the field is rich and psychological theory and research continue to be applied across the criminological and legal fields. One of the challenges for those who work in this area is the range of material with which they must be familiar before advancing into the real world. I find myself reading almost as much criminology and law as I do psychology books and journals. There are, I think, a number of advantages in reading seriously across disciplines. For example, one reads criticism of psychological research from outside main-stream psychology. This outside view, so to speak, sharpens one's own criti-cal faculties in both the theoretical and applied domains. However, there is a sense that currently the application of research is outstripping the develop-ment of theory. The next fundamental step to be taken is to attempt a meta-theoretical explanation of criminal behaviour, incorporating what is known from criminological, legal, and psychological research. The impact of such a meta-theory on forensic practice *would* be interesting to behold.

FURTHER READING

Gudjonsson, G. (1992). *The psychology of interrogations, confessions and testimony.* Chichester: Wiley.

Hollin, C. R. (1989). *Psychology and crime: An introduction to criminological psychology.* London: Routledge.

Kagehiro, D. K., & Laufer, W. S. (Eds) (1992). *Handbook of psychology and law.* New York: Springer-Verlag.

Quay, H. C. (Ed.) (1987). *Handbook of juvenile delinquency.* New York: Wiley.

Weiner, I. B., & Hess, A. K. (Eds) (1987). *Handbook of forensic psychology.* New York: Wiley.

REFERENCES

Akers, R. L. (1990). Rational choice, deterrence, and social learning theory in crim-inology: The path not taken. *Journal of Criminal Law and Criminology, 81,* 653–676.

Andrews, D. A. (1990). Some criminological sources of anti-rehabilitation bias in the Report of the Canadian Sentencing Commission. *Canadian Journal of Criminology, 2,* 511–524.

Andrews, D. A., Zinger, I., Hoge, R. D., Bonta, J., Gendreau, P., & Cullen, F. T. (1990). Does correctional treatment work? A clinically relevant and informed meta-analysis. *Criminology, 28,* 369–404.

Bandura, A. (1977). *Social learning theory.* Englewood Cliffs, NJ: Prentice-Hall.

Brantingham, P. L., & Brantingham, P. J. (1990). Situational crime prevention in practice. *Canadian Journal of Criminology, 32,* 17–40.

Brigham, J. C., Maass, A., Snyder, L. D., & Spaulding, K. (1982). Accuracy of eyewitness identification in a field setting. *Journal of Personality and Social Psychology*, *42*, 673–681.

Burrows, J. (1980). Closed circuit television and crime on the London Underground. In R. V. G. Clarke & P. Mayhew (Eds) *Designing out crime* (pp. 75–83). London: Her Majesty's Stationery Office.

Colman, A. M. (1991). Crowd psychology in South African murder trials. *American Psychologist*, *46*, 1071–1079.

Cornish, D. B., & Clarke, R. V. G. (Eds) (1986). *The reasoning criminal: Rational choice perspectives on crime*. New York: Springer-Verlag.

Cullen, F. T., & Gendreau, P. (1989). The effectiveness of correctional rehabilitation: Reconsidering the "nothing works" debate. In L. Goodstein & D. L. MacKenzie (Eds) *The American prison: Issues in research and policy* (pp. 23–44). New York: Plenum.

Cutler, B. L., & Penrod, S. D. (1988). Improving the reliability of eyewitness identification: Lineup construction and presentation. *Journal of Applied Psychology*, *73*, 281–290.

Davies, G. M. (1983). Forensic face recall: The role of visual and verbal information. In S. M. A. Lloyd-Bostock & B. R. Clifford (Eds) *Evaluating witness evidence: Recent psychological research and new perspectives* (pp. 103–123). Chichester: Wiley.

Davies, G. M. (1986). Capturing likeness in eyewitness composites: The police artist and his rivals. *Medicine, Science and the Law*, *26*, 283–290.

Diamond, S. S. (1992). Foreword. In D. K. Kagehiro & W. S. Laufer (Eds) *Handbook of psychology and law* (pp. v–ix). New York: Springer-Verlag.

Dodge, K. A. (1986). A social-information processing model of social competence in children. In M. Permutter (Ed.) *Minnesota symposium on child psychology* (vol. 18, pp. 77–125). Hillsdale, NJ: Lawrence Erlbaum.

Fisher, R. P., Geiselman, R. E., & Amador, M. (1989). Field test of the cognitive interview: Enhancing the recollection of actual victims and witnesses of crime. *Journal of Applied Psychology*, *74*, 722–727.

Freedman, B. J., Rosenthal, L., Donahue, C. P., Schlundt, D. G., & McFall, R. M. (1978). A social-behavioral analysis of skills deficits in delinquent and non-delinquent adolescent boys. *Journal of Consulting and Clinical Psychology*, *46*, 1448–1462.

Garrett, C. J. (1985). Effects of residential treatment of adjudicated delinquents: A meta-analysis. *Journal of Research in Crime and Delinquency*, *22*, 287–308.

Gendreau, P., & Andrews, D. A. (1990). Tertiary prevention: What the meta-analyses of the offender treatment literature tell us about "what works". *Canadian Journal of Criminology*, *32*, 173–184.

Gendreau, P., & Ross, R. R. (1979). Effective correctional treatment: Bibliotherapy for cynics. *Crime and Delinquency*, *25*, 463–489.

Gendreau, P., & Ross, R. R. (1987). Revivification of rehabilitation: Evidence from the 1980s. *Justice Quarterly*, *4*, 349–407.

Goodman, G. S., & Hahn, A. (1987). Evaluating eyewitness testimony. In I. B. Weiner & A. K. Hess (Eds) *Handbook of forensic psychology* (pp. 258–292). New York: Wiley.

Gudjonsson, G. (1992). *The psychology of interrogations, confessions and testimony*. Chichester: Wiley.

Gudjonsson, G., & Clark, N. K. (1986). Suggestibility in police interrogation: A social psychological model. *Social Behaviour*, *1*, 83–104.

Hans, V. P. (1992). Jury decision making. In D. K. Kagehiro & W. S. Laufer (Eds) *Handbook of psychology and law* (pp. 56–76). New York: Springer-Verlag.

Hans, V. P., & Vidmar, N. (1986). *Judging the jury*. New York: Plenum.

Heal, K., & Laycock, G. (Eds) (1986). *Situational crime prevention: From theory into practice*. London: Her Majesty's Stationery Office.

Hollin, C. R. (1989). *Psychology and crime: An introduction to criminological psychology*. London: Routledge.

Hollin, C. R. (1990a). Social skills training with delinquents: A look at the evidence and some recommendations for practice. *British Journal of Social Work, 20*, 483–493.

Hollin, C. R. (1990b). *Cognitive-behavioral interventions with young offenders*. Elmsford, NY: Pergamon.

Hollin, C. R. (1992). *Criminal behaviour: A psychological approach to explanation and prevention*. London: Falmer.

Hollin, C. R., & Henderson, M. (1984). Social skills training with young offenders: False expectations and the "failure of treatment". *Behavioural Psychotherapy, 12*, 331–341.

Hollin, C. R., & Wheeler, H. M. (1982). The violent young offender: A small group study of a Borstal population. *Journal of Adolescence, 5*, 247–257.

Huff, C. R., & Rattner, A. (1988). Convicted but innocent: False positives and the criminal justice process. In E. Scott & T. Hirschi (Eds) *Controversial issues in crime and justice* (pp. 130–144). Beverly Hills, CA: Sage.

Inbau, F. E., Reid, J. E., & Buckley, J. P. (1986). *Criminal interrogation and confessions* (3rd edn). Baltimore, MD: Williams & Wilkins.

Izzo, R. L., & Ross, R. R. (1990). Meta-analysis of rehabilitation programs for juvenile delinquents: A brief report. *Criminal Justice and Behavior, 17*, 134–142.

Jeffery, C. R. (1965). Criminal behavior and learning theory. *Journal of Criminal Law, Criminology and Police Science, 56*, 294–300.

Kagehiro, D. K., & Laufer, W. S. (Eds) (1992). *Handbook of psychology and law*. New York: Springer-Verlag.

Kassin, S. M., & Wrightsman, L. S. (1985). Confession evidence. In S. M. Kassin & L. S. Wrightsman (Eds) *The psychology of evidence and trial procedure* (pp. 67–94). Beverly Hills, CA: Sage.

Linz, D., & Penrod, S. (1992). Exploring the First and Sixth Amendments: Pretrial publicity and jury decision making. In D. K. Kagehiro & W. S. Laufer (Eds) *Handbook of psychology and law* (pp. 3–36). New York: Springer-Verlag.

Lipsey, M. W. (1992). Juvenile delinquency treatment: A meta-analytic inquiry into the variability of effects. In T. D. Cook, H. Cooper, D. S. Cordray, H. Hartmann, L. V. Hedges, R. J. Light, T. A. Louis, & F. Mosteller (Eds) *Meta-analysis for explanation: A casebook* (pp. 83–127). New York: Russell Sage Foundation.

Lloyd-Bostock, S. M. A. (1988). *Law in practice*. London: British Psychological Society and Routledge.

Lloyd-Bostock, S. M. A., & Clifford, B. R. (Eds) (1983). *Evaluating witness evidence: Recent psychological research and new perspectives*. Chichester: Wiley.

Loftus, E. F., & Ketcham, K. E. (1983). The malleability of eyewitness accounts. In S. M. A. Lloyd-Bostock & B. R. Clifford (Eds) *Evaluating eyewitness evidence: Recent psychological research and new perspectives* (pp. 159–171). Chichester: Wiley.

Martinson, R. (1974). What works? Questions and answers about prison reform. *Public Interest, 35*, 22–54.

Martinson, R. (1979). New findings, new views: A note of caution regarding sentencing reform. *Hofsta Law Review, 7*, 242–258.

Maxfield, M. G., & Baumer, T. L. (1990). Home detention with electronic monitoring: Comparing pretrial and postconviction programs. *Crime and Delinquency*, *36*, 521–536.

Mayhew, P., Elliott, D., & Dowds, L. (1989). *The 1988 British Crime Survey*. London: Her Majesty's Stationery Office.

Münsterberg, H. (1908). *On the witness stand: Essays on psychology and crime*. New York: Clark, Boardman.

Nellis, M. (1991). The electronic monitoring of offenders in England and Wales. *British Journal of Criminology*, *31*, 165–185.

Nelson, J. R., Smith, D. J., & Dodd, J. (1990). The moral reasoning of juvenile delinquents: A meta-analysis. *Journal of Abnormal Child Psychology*, *18*, 231–239.

Novaco, R. W., & Welsh, W. N. (1989). Anger disturbances: Cognitive mediation and clinical prescriptions. In K. Howells & C. R. Hollin (Eds) *Clinical approaches to violence* (pp. 39–60). Chichester: Wiley.

Penrod, S. D., & Cutler, B. L. (1987). Assessing the competence of juries. In I. B. Weiner & A. K. Hess (Eds) *Handbook of forensic psychology* (pp. 293–318). New York: Wiley.

Quay, H. C. (Ed.) (1987). *Handbook of juvenile delinquency*. New York: Wiley.

Raskin, D. C. (Ed.) (1989). *Psychological methods in criminal investigation and evidence*. New York: Springer.

Roberts, A. R., & Camasso, M. J. (1991). The effect of juvenile offender treatment programs on recidivism: A meta-analysis of 46 studies. *Notre Dame Journal of Law, Ethics and Public Policy*, *5*, 421–441.

Roshier, B. (1989). *Controlling crime: The classical perspective in criminology*. Milton Keynes: Open University Press.

Ross, R. R., & Fabiano, E. A. (1985). *Time to think: A cognitive model of delinquency prevention and offender rehabilitation*. Johnson City, TN: Institute of Social Sciences and Arts.

Sanders, G. S., & Warnick, D. H. (1981). Truth and consequences: The effect of responsibility on eyewitness behavior. *Basic and Applied Social Psychology*, *2*, 67–79.

Slaby, R. G., & Guerra, N. G. (1988). Cognitive mediators of aggression in adolescent offenders: 1. Assessment. *Developmental Psychology*, *24*, 580–588.

Sutherland, E. H. (1939). *Principles of criminology*. Philadelphia, PA: Lippincott.

Thornton, D. M. (1987). Treatment effects on recidivism: A reappraisal of the "nothing works" doctrine. In B. J. McGurk, D. M. Thornton, & M. Williams (Eds) *Applying psychology to imprisonment: Theory and practice* (pp. 181–189). London: Her Majesty's Stationery Office.

Thornton, D. M., & Reid, R. L. (1982). Moral reasoning and type of criminal offence. *British Journal of Social Psychology*, *21*, 231–238.

Wells, G. L. (1986). Expert psychological testimony: Empirical and conceptual analyses of effects. *Law and Human Behavior*, *10*, 83–95.

Wells, G. L., & Loftus, E. F. (Eds) (1984). *Eyewitness testimony: Psychological perspectives*. Cambridge: Cambridge University Press.

West, D. J. (1980). The clinical approach to criminology. *Psychological Medicine*, *10*, 619–631.

Williams, K. D., Loftus, E. F., & Deffenbacher, K. A. (1992). Eyewitness evidence and testimony. In D. K. Kagehiro & W. S. Laufer (Eds) *Handbook of psychology and law* (pp. 141–166). New York: Springer-Verlag.

Yarmey, A. D. (1979). *The psychology of eyewitness testimony*. New York: Free Press.

Yuille, J. C., & Cutshall, J. L. (1986). A case study of eyewitness memory to a crime. *Journal of Applied Psychology, 71*, 291–301.

Zaragoza, M. S., McCluskey, M., & Jarvis, M. (1987). Misleading post-event information and recall of the original event: Further evidence against the memory impairment hypothesis. *Journal of Experimental Psychology: Learning, Memory and Cognition, 13*, 36–44.

5

PSYCHOANALYSIS

Peter Fonagy
University College London, England

The development of	Fairbairn and Winnicott
psychoanalytic theory	Kohut's theory
The affect trauma model	**Psychoanalysis**
The topographical model	**Psychoanalytic psychotherapy**
The structural model	**Evaluation**
Post-Freudian psychoanalysis	**Further reading**
Ego psychology	**References**
Melanie Klein and her	
followers	

Psychoanalysis is at least four things. First and foremost, it is a method of psychotherapeutic treatment originated by two Viennese physicians, Joseph Breuer and Sigmund Freud, who first described "the talking cure" in their visionary book *Studies on Hysteria* published in 1895. It was elaborated and extended in the corpus of Freud's work as well as that of psychoanalysts who followed him.

The psychoanalytic method is deceptively simple. Two people meet daily for a set period of time, usually 50 minutes, in surroundings designed to minimize extraneous stimuli. Traditionally the room has a couch on which the analysand (the patient) can lie comfortably and a chair for the analyst, who normally sits out of range of the patient's vision. The analysand speaks spontaneously of whatever is passing through his or her mind. Analysts normally restrict themselves to listening, and they try to make sense of what they hear and observe and communicate their conclusions to the patient from time to time.

Among the techniques described by Freud as part of psychoanalysis are *free association* (encouraging patients to tell their therapist all their thoughts without attempt at censorship) and *interpretation* (the attempt on the part of the therapist to identify feelings, links, and ideas in the patient's verbalization of which the patient was unaware). Other phenomena that serve the psychoanalytic process are *transference* (the tendency of patients to re-experience, in the context of the therapeutic relationship, their feelings and conflicts associated with early caregiving figures) and *insight* (the curative effect of arriving at a conscious understanding of the unconscious and mostly childlike reasons that underlie maladaptive behaviour). Psychoanalysis is a form of therapy that is at the same time a source of psychological data. Psychoanalysts use their clinical experience with patients as a basis for generalizations about psychopathology, personality, and human psychology.

Second, psychoanalysis is a theory of mental illness, particularly of neurosis. It holds that many maladaptive behaviours, such as anxiety or depression, for which individuals seek psychological help, are symptoms of a dysfunctional mental system. More specifically, symptoms serve to help the individual to resolve conflicts between conscious and non-conscious feelings, ideas, and fantasies. For example, the neurotic symptom of depression may represent a way of avoiding conscious confrontation with a much-loved figure towards whom the individual unconsciously experiences feelings of violent rage. If anger in connection with that individual is felt to be intolerable – perhaps the object of the anger is perceived as fragile or as potentially dangerous – the person may resolve the conflict by turning the anger against him- or herself. The result will be the experience of pervasive self-criticism, a sense of total inadequacy, and a painful sense of worthlessness.

Third, psychoanalysis is a theory of individual differences and personality. It is constructed to account for differences in character that we all observe in people we know: family, friends, and colleagues. Why is one person more self-assured, confident, and apparently unconcerned about criticism than another? The psychoanalytic account of such differences would reach into the nature of early relationships that individuals had with their primary caregivers. People who are diffident and constantly in need of reassurance and praise might have had parental figures who were less attentive or simply less perceptive of their early childhood achievements. They have had no opportunity to internalize the ability to judge the value of actions, and consequently they remain uncertain of the worth of their achievements despite considerable evidence to the contrary (that is, their past history of significant personal accomplishments). They thus find themselves constantly turning to the outside world for an affirmation of the appropriateness of their actions. Psychoanalysts have made considerable efforts to draw up a typology of human character and to provide explanations, in terms of common patterns of childhood experience and reactions to these, for individual differences in personality.

Fourth, psychoanalysis is a psychology; it is a collection of theories or generalizations made about the functioning of human minds based on psychoanalytic clinical experience. Freud and his followers constructed a model of the mind, consistent with their clinical experience, which has been very influential in general psychology. Freud drew attention to the limited access that the conscious mind has to all the mental processes one needs to postulate to provide an adequate account of human behaviour. He likened the mind to an iceberg, and awareness to its very tip, the only part of the structure above the waterline. He also conceived of the need for mechanisms of psychological defence, mental operations, with the function of reducing anxiety. Thus he noted that we often choose to forget aspects of our life that carry painful connotations, and he hypothesised that this phenomenon was underpinned by the defensive manoeuvre of repression.

Finally, psychoanalysis also encompasses Freud's most ambitious project. He intended it to be a general theory of human civilization with the potential to enrich the description of social phenomena and cultural products and codes, in addition to being a psychology of the unconscious and a theory of individual differences and psychopathology. For example, he contemplated the nature of humour, in particular jokes. He noted that rarely, if ever, are jokes genuinely innocent, free of sexual or aggressive innuendo. He proposed that jokes permit a temporary suspension of culturally imposed constraints on human thoughts, fantasies, and emotions and thus bypass the forces of repression. Perhaps this is why it is notoriously difficult to remember jokes. We hear literally thousands of jokes and humorous remarks over the course of our lives, yet most of us find it well-nigh impossible to recall successfully more than a handful of genuinely funny stories.

Freud also commented on art. He was convinced that psychoanalysts, through their understanding of the individual psyche, achieved unique insights into aesthetic experience. Through art the contents of the unconscious mind can be communicated rapidly and in all its complexity, and aesthetic experience is the appreciation of the artist's ability to perform this remarkable feat.

THE DEVELOPMENT OF PSYCHOANALYTIC THEORY

Not surprisingly, psychoanalysis has undergone several major transformations between its inception in the late nineteenth century and its current form nearly 100 years later. What makes this development somewhat difficult to follow is that these changes to psychoanalytic ideas tend not to be transformations or substitutions of one theoretical framework for another. Rather, new ideas were added to old ones, enriching existing theoretical frameworks and developing alternative formulations, but stopping short of discarding previous proposals. The end result is a body of knowledge containing very many inherent contradictions and inconsistencies.

This is one of the greatest weaknesses of psychoanalytic epistemology;

psychoanalysis seems unable to discard plausible ideas once proposed and accepted, even if alternative formulations would provide a better account of the same phenomenon. Psychoanalysts have become accustomed to this state of affairs, and psychoanalysis is taught in most institutes in a historical manner, starting with Freud's earliest ideas and building up to more recent formulations. I shall follow this tradition.

The affect trauma model

Freud's first major psychoanalytic proposal concerned the nature of hysteria. This is a condition in which the patient experiences physical symptoms, for example blindness or paralysis, without obvious organic cause. Breuer and Freud (1895) discovered that such symptoms were not due to the degeneration of the nervous system (as previously thought), but rather were frequently responses to a major emotional trauma of which the patient appeared to have no conscious knowledge. The experiences were of such emotional force that the patient's mind failed in its attempt to exclude the experience from consciousness, and the affect associated with the trauma broke through and manifested as the symptom which had hidden connections to the original experience. For example, a 45-year-old man suffered temporary unexplained blindness after witnessing his wife having sex with his best friend.

Freud's idea was less than popular; this was primarily because he dared to suggest that, most commonly, hysterical symptoms are the consequence of the psychic trauma associated with the physical or sexual abuse of children. More recently, it has become generally accepted that, in the majority of cases of severe personality disorder of the kind discussed by Freud at this time, childhood maltreatment *is* an important causal factor.

One of several reasons for the failure of Freud's early formulation was the inadequacy of the treatment. Freud's therapy involved the release of pent-up emotion (catharsis) associated with early trauma by helping patients to bring the experience fully into consciousness (abreaction). Freud attempted to use hypnosis to achieve this effect, but it was a method in which he was not particularly proficient. Abreaction and catharsis, abandoned for many years by psychotherapists, are once again key components in many current treatments of post-traumatic stress disorder.

The topographical model

By 1900, Freud had discarded his childhood-seduction theory, constructed a new general model of mental function, revised his theory of neurotic disturbance, and laid down the principles of psychoanalytic treatment as described above. The corner-stone of Freud's (1900) new theory was the assumption that much human thought inevitably takes place outside consciousness. He distinguished the conscious, preconscious, and unconscious systems of the mind. Psychological difficulties could be explained by a conflict between unconsciously held, childlike wishes and the largely socially acceptable ideas which constitute the contents of consciousness.

He postulated that sexual and aggressive mental contents are repudiated by consciousness. These arise out of instinct-driven motives and dominate the *System Unconscious*. The *System Preconscious* is the middle layer within this topographical model and plays a primary role in the distortion and censorship of forbidden instinctual wishes; it permits thoughts from the *System Unconscious* to access consciousness only if they are already so distorted that their unconscious origins can no longer be detected.

Freud's (1905) dual instinct theory postulated a sexual and, later, an aggressive drive. The individual was seen by Freud as "defending" against aggressive and sexual wishes by *repressing* them into the non-conscious part of the mind. Repression was assumed not to function under certain conditions and these permitted insight into the functioning of the unconscious.

During sleep, the part of the mind responsible for protecting consciousness from unacceptable impulses (which Freud called the censor) weakens in its function; thus the mental content of sleep (the dream) contains more or less direct reflections of unconscious mental contents. Repressed wishes find expression through dreams, albeit in an indirect form. Thus the dream of a small child about losing a favourite pet might be interpreted as an expression of an unconscious wish to "lose", or at any rate to be rid of, a younger sibling.

Freud realized that the conscious contemplation of instinct-driven wishes would create anxiety; hence the need for repression and censorship even in dreams. The expression of forbidden impulses in dreams may explain why most of our dreams are associated with the experience of anxiety and are distorted to circumvent understanding by the censor. The mode of thinking in the System Unconscious was seen by Freud as fundamentally different from conscious thought. The unconscious was assumed to be dominated by primary process thinking: impulsive, disorganized, and bizarre visual images, untroubled by considerations of time, order, or logical consistency. Freud claimed that the bizarre, irrational nature of dreams reflected the functioning of primary thought processes and could be understood if the mechanisms of distortion were carefully unravelled. Freud (1900) reported a dream he had had of seeing his sleeping mother being carried into a room by some bird-headed people. Freud interpreted the dream as a disguised expression of his sexual feelings for his mother. The word for bird (*Vogel*) is similar to the German slang word for having sex (*vögeln*).

Unconscious wishes are also directly expressed in jokes. It is hard to think of genuinely humorous stories that do not involve a certain degree of aggressive content which, outside the permissive atmosphere created by humour, would be totally unacceptable. Slips of the tongue – also called "Freudian slips' – may occasionally directly express unconscious concerns.

For example, a US woman senator spoke in highly indignant terms about ideological repression in the United States "of feminists, homosexuals, and other perversions – I mean persuasions".

Freud (1905) constructed a view of human life determined by primitive human urges that we need to master, over the first years of life, in order to conform to the demands of society. These drives were assumed to be rooted in the body; their mental representation occurs in terms of the wish for gratification directed towards external figures (objects). The biological evolution of the instinct over the course of life provided the principal framework for the psychoanalytic theory of development. The sexual instinct was thought to develop through a predictable sequence of stages marked by specific bodily concerns.

The early stages of psychosexual development were assumed by Freud to be organized around oral pleasures and anal concerns. In the fourth and fifth years of life the child is thought to enter into a particularly formative phase. Children develop close ties with the caregiver which they wish to maintain as an exclusive bond. Their increased cognitive awareness leads them to consider other individuals, particularly siblings and the other parent, as threatening the exclusivity of the relationship to the primary caretaker.

Freud's notion of the *Oedipus complex* concerns the child's feelings about the other parent, this "third" potentially rivalrous figure. Classically, the little boy's exclusive relationship with his mother is threatened by the father's presence, which leads the little boy to harbour powerful unconscious feelings of hostility towards his rival. His fear of retaliation leads him to identify with his father instead of opposing him. A similar process is thought to take place for girls, although the fear of retribution in girls is less intense than in boys, with the result that Oedipal attitudes tend to be less strongly repressed in women, and the father remains a sexually attractive figure.

Pre-eminent in Freud's view of neurosis at this time was the individual's need to maintain unconscious wishes and drives outside consciousness. He made an important distinction between neurotic symptoms and character traits. While the latter owe their existence to a successful defence against instinctual impulses, neurotic symptoms come into being as a result of the failure of repression. When sexual drives find expression they create anxiety or guilt.

The First World War led Freud to broaden his theory of drives to include primary aggression as well as sexuality. He concluded that much of human behaviour, including the destructiveness of war, and crimes of people against one another, could not be explained unless some basic aggressive destructive drive were postulated. Indeed, subsequent events have shown all too clearly the precariousness of human civilization when confronted with basic human motives of territoriality, vengefulness, bigotry, and self-interest. Throughout the evolution of psychoanalytic theory, the concept of anxiety-producing wishes, experiences, and desires that are pushed from conscious awareness but re-emerge in neurotic symptoms has remained constant.

The structural model

Freud gradually realized that there was more to mental functioning than could be encompassed in a simple distinction between unconscious, preconscious, and conscious mental processes. In 1923 he spelt out the structural viewpoint of psychoanalysis in *The Ego and the Id*. This work for the first time integrated Freud's concepts of drives, defences, and affects, and indicated his aspiration to provide a fully-fledged general psychology rather than a theory of maladjustment. He described three sets of mental processes or structures.

The first, entirely unconscious structure, the id, is the reservoir of sexual and aggressive drives.

The second structure, the superego, was seen as the organized psychic representation of childhood parental authority figures. The child's picture of his or her parents is naturally not realistic. The internalized authority figure is far stricter and harsher in most cases than the parents would actually have been. The superego contains both the goals and the aspirations derived from parents and society (the ego ideal) and the self-corrective functions mediated by guilt. Guilt is an unpleasant sensation, or affect, and individuals do much, including resisting the instinctual aggressive and sexual pressures of the id, in order to avoid being overwhelmed by it.

The third component of the model is the ego. The ego encapsulates mental processes such as thinking, memory, and perception, which collectively enable the individual to cope with the demands and restrictions of external reality. The ego mediates initially between the drives and reality, and later on, as moral sense develops, between the drives and the superego.

This new model represented an extension of Freud's thinking in a number of ways. First, social acceptability was no longer synonymous with consciousness. In this view, most sophisticated psychological processes could function without the benefit of consciousness. Second, anxiety which was previously seen by Freud as undischarged sexual energy was here seen as a signal of danger arising within the ego whenever external demands or internal impulses represented a major threat. This might occur under the danger of loss of love or of enormous guilt as well as danger of physical injury.

The identification of defence mechanisms was one of Freud's early achievements, but it was not until the advent of the structural model that their function and organization could be elaborated adequately. Defences were seen by Freud and his daughter Anna Freud as unconscious mental processes mediated within the ego to prevent the development of painful affect, particularly anxiety or guilt.

Defence mechanisms involve distortions of the way an individual perceives

82

and experiences aspects of his world. *Reaction formation* is a mechanism that serves to maintain repression by intensifying its antithesis. For instance, people disturbed by cruel impulses towards animals might find it helpful to offer their services to the Royal Society for the Prevention of Cruelty to Animals. This would protect them from expressing aggressive impulses by channelling all their energies into preserving rather than destroying life.

Other defence mechanisms include *denial* (refusal to acknowledge that an event has occurred or is likely to occur, for example that one has a terminal illness); *displacement* (transfer of affect from one person or situation to another); *isolation* (splitting feelings off from thought, for example immediately following severe trauma); *suppression* (the conscious decision to avoid attending to anxiety- or guilt-provoking circumstances); *sublimation* (the gratifying of an instinctual impulse by giving it a socially acceptable aim, for example sublimated aggression in violent sports); *regression* (reversion to a childlike manner of behaving that was safe, acceptable, and gratifying); *acting out* (allowing direct expression of an unconscious impulse, for example by slips of the tongue); and *intellectualization* (separating a threatening impulse from its emotional context and placing it in a sometimes inappropriate, rational framework).

Psychopathology is substantially more complex in the structural model than it was within the topographical view. In the structural model the neurotic symptom is seen as representing a combination of unacceptable impulses which threaten to overwhelm the ego and the defences utilized by the individual against them. Anxiety, the hallmark of most neurotic reaction types, was seen by Freud as the reaction of the ego, signalling its imminent danger of being overwhelmed and mobilizing its defensive capabilities. An often-quoted analogy compares anxiety to a fire alarm, set off at the first sign of smoke, aimed at summoning the assistance of the fire brigade. The neurotic reaction types are distinguished by the manner in which the ego defends itself against the anxiety and guilt engendered by childhood instinctual impulses. Thus, in phobias Freud saw the operation of the mechanisms of projection and displacement. A little boy projects his own envious and jealous anger on to his father because it is inconsistent with the love and fear he also feels. The projection of these feelings distorts the boy's perception of his father and he begins to see him as a murderously angry man. This experience may also be too painful and frightening to bear, particularly if he is a lovable and valued object to the child. The fear is then displaced on to objects with whom he has less intimate ties: thus he may become terrified of burglars whom he fears may come to kill him during the night. A paranoid person was thought to use reaction-formation as a defence against conflictual homosexual impulses. "I love him" turns into "I hate him", which by projection becomes "He hates me". These early psychoanalytic theories of homosexuality have been the subject of substantial revision.

In obsessive-compulsive neurosis, Freud thought that individuals defend against aggressive impulses by reaction-formation. Thus they might turn the feared wish to murder brutally, for example, into endless worry over the safety of the person concerned. Sometimes the aggression is fended off by isolation, so that individuals continue to experience the violent images consciously but feel that they are bizarre, do not belong, and are being thrust upon them from outside.

POST-FREUDIAN PSYCHOANALYSIS

Following Freud's death, psychoanalytic thought developed in two fundamentally different ways. In the United States, and to a lesser extent in Britain, certain psychoanalysts grew dissatisfied with the limitations of Freud's approach. These analysts tried to elaborate further the functioning of the ego, focusing on those parts not actively involved in the struggles with the id or the superego. Meanwhile, mainly in Britain, another group of analysts worked on the effects of early relationships, especially those between the infant and his mother. Many other important theorists developed new ideas from Freud's work, those of Jung, Horney, Sullivan, and Adler being examples. Later, however, the most prolific theorists were in the areas of *ego psychology* and various *object-relations theories*.

Ego psychology

Heinz Hartmann (1958) originated a new psychoanalytic approach based on the study of the ego which he felt was a notion neglected by Freud. The central theme of Hartmann's conception was that the ego is not solely involved in conflicts with warring internal structures but is also able to function independently of drives or of involvement in conflicts. The ego was seen as capable, given an adequate environment, of perceiving, learning, remembering, thinking, moving, acting, organizing, synthesizing, and achieving a balance. These capabilities were referred to as the autonomous functions of the ego.

From this background, Erikson (1959) proposed a psychosocial model of ego development. He emphasized the notion of developmental crises. These were held to occur at each of eight stages of development (corresponding in part to Freud's psychosexual stages but taking into account also the problems of transition to early, middle, and late adulthood) and arose from the individual's need to adapt to changed circumstances and social expectations brought about through the process of maturation.

Each crisis is characterized by its own pair of opposing (desirable and undesirable) personality traits (for example, the stage of basic trustfulness versus mistrustfulness from birth to 18 months). With the resolution of each crisis, the individual acquires a relatively permanent balance between the desirable and undesirable traits designating that stage. Among all of

Erikson's stages, the stage of adolescent crisis (the opposition of identity and role confusion) has made most impact.

A major innovation introduced by Hartmann concerns the gratification available to the organism from the sheer exercise of its functions (for example the pleasure a child gains from learning to walk or draw). Additionally, ego psychologists (notably Rapaport, 1967) emphasized that the seeking of stimuli, described as a search for novelty (or curiosity), is necessary for normal development. This enabled some psychoanalysts to move away from Freud's severely criticized motivational system (cf. G. S. Klein, 1976), which had tension-reduction as its sole aim. In the current psychoanalytic view, the ego is a balance-inducing system striving to find an optimal level of tension, using induction as well as reduction.

Ego psychology has undoubtedly been the most influential psychoanalytic model in the United States. Furthermore, of all the major psychoanalytic approaches it has come the closest to achieving a unification with general psychology; yet since the 1970s it has met with a substantial amount of criticism as being confused and conceptually inadequate. Holt (1976) called instinct theory, which remained a corner-stone of ego psychology, the "shame of psychoanalysis", so riddled was it with philosophical and factual errors and fallacies that nothing short of discarding the concept would do. George Klein (1976) recommended the abandonment of all of psychoanalytic theory not directly concerned with the understanding of clinical problems presented by psychoanalytic clients. It was felt by some that psychoanalytic theory should abandon any claim to identify general psychological structures and mechanisms such as the ego and instincts and apply itself to clinical problems only. Perhaps in response to these inadequacies of the ego psychological approach, US analysts are increasingly turning to the British tradition of psychoanalytic thought.

Melanie Klein and her followers

Developments in Britain and most recent developments in the United States represent a movement away from the formal mechanistic framework of structures, forces, and energies that characterized Freud's structural model and Hartmann's ego psychology. The move is towards a more clinically oriented theory, primarily concerned with the development of infants, their sense of self, their relationships with their caregivers (their objects), and the implications of the internal representations of such relationships on future development. Thus psychoanalytic attention has shifted to the examination of self-other relationships using a language much closer to that of day-to-day experience. Melanie Klein's (1932, 1948) approach is chiefly distinguished by being the first to emphasize the importance of infants' earliest relationships. In developing Freud's ideas, she discovered that children's play could be interpreted in a way similar to that used to interpret the verbal associations of adults.

Perhaps the most far-reaching of her theoretical contributions has been her insistence that neurosis has its origins in the first year of life. The main source of difficulty at this stage is the infant's innate ambivalence about his or her most important object relationship: the nourishing but sometimes frustrating breast. A basic assumption of Klein's theory was that from their earliest times infants' mental lives are dominated by unbearable conflicts between love (the manifestation of the libido) and hate (the aggressive instinct). This conflict is reduced, and a feeling of safety promoted, by putting or projecting the aggressive impulses into the breast. However, in this way the breast could also at times become a frightening and dangerous object for them. At other times, the breast was felt as good, was cherished and loved.

Klein called the normal working-through by infants of their fear and suspicion of the breast the "paranoid-schizoid position". During the second half of the first year the painful discovery is made that the loved and the hated breasts are one and the same object. Klein maintained that until the infant could become confident of being loved in spite of his/her rage, every occasion when the breast was removed would be interpreted by the infant as a loss due to the infant's own destructive fantasies. This would be accompanied by feelings of sadness, guilt, and regret. Klein believed that all infants go through this repeated experience of sorrow for the loved object, fear of losing it, and then longing to regain it. The infant can get beyond this "depressive position" only when assured of having maternal love. The infant needs to accept responsibility for the destructive fantasies and follow this by mental acts of reparation (sorrow and sadness); only then would the depressive position be overcome. Klein explained later psychological disturbance less in terms of actual experiences than the internal experience of infancy, in which unconscious fantasies and wishes predominate. If the depressive position was not adequately negotiated in infancy, the individual would never succeed in establishing a stable internal image of a good and loving object. There would be a predisposition to return to the depressive position with consequent feelings of loss, sorrow, guilt, anxiety, and low self-esteem: in other words, such individuals would be likely to feel insufficiently loved and would be particularly prone to depression and other psychological problems.

Kleinian theory has been very influential in British psychoanalysis (Spillius, 1988) and is receiving increasing attention in the United States. Kleinian writers since the early 1950s have worked to understand the mental processes underlying psychotic disturbance, where the patient loses the capacity reliably to distinguish reality from fantasy, and severe character pathology such as borderline states characterized by poor interpersonal relationships, violent changes of mood, impulsivity, and self-destructiveness.

Kernberg's (1975, 1984) highly influential psychostructural model emphasizes the inevitability of psychic conflict and its by-products of anxiety, guilt, and shame in the course of early human development. The root cause of severe personality disturbance, such as borderline states, in Kernberg's model is the intensity of destructive and aggressive impulses and the relative weakness of ego structures available to handle them. Kernberg sees such individuals as using developmentally early defences in an attempt to separate contradictory images of self and others, in order to protect positive images from being overwhelmed by negative and hostile ones. The infant's attempts to protect the object from destruction with the only rudimentary psychic mechanisms at his or her disposal, leads to the defensive fragmentation of self and object representations. Later manifestations of the borderline condition therefore represent a developmentally unresolved infantile conflict state. These conflicts may reasonably be expected to continue within the context of treatment and their interpretation is assumed to have therapeutic effects.

Kernberg's approach has much in common with followers of Melanie Klein (Bion, 1957; Klein, 1957; Segal, 1964) who also stress the inevitability of pathological sequelae arising out of innate destructiveness. The crucial difference lies in later Kleinian thinking (see Spillius, 1988) concerning the common defensive organization that appears to exist in much borderline pathology. The term "organization" – for example narcissistic organization (Rosenfeld, 1987; Sohn, 1985), defensive organization (O'Shaughnessy, 1981), pathological organization (Steiner, 1987) – refers to a relatively firm construction of impulses, anxieties, and defences, creating stability, but at the expense of more advanced modes of psychic functioning which would lead to intolerable depressive anxiety. The psychic defences work together in an extremely rigid system making therapeutic progress difficult and rarely entirely successful. It is as if the psychic structure itself becomes the embodiment of the destructive impulses which called it into existence in the first place. Bion (1962) provides one explanation. He sees the ego's identification with an object, felt to be full of envy and hate, as resulting in an early disabling of certain psychic processes having to do with the capacity to understand cognitive and affective aspects of interpersonal relationships.

Kernberg (1967, 1975, 1976, 1984) conceived of borderline personality disorder as a level of psychic functioning referred to as borderline personality organization. In this respect he continued Melanie Klein's emphasis on defensive personality organization. The borderline personality organization, according to Kernberg, rests on four critical features of the patient's personality-structure: first, non-specific manifestations of ego weakness, including difficulty in tolerating anxiety, controlling impulses, or developing socially productive ways of channelling energy (sublimation); second, a propensity to shift towards irrational, dream-like thinking patterns in the context of generally intact reality-testing; third, predominance of early psychological defences such as splitting, projection, and projective identification; fourth, diffusion of identity, and the related pathology of internal object relations, such that mental representations of important others are fragmented and strongly charged as either good or bad. Thus Kernberg's concept of borderline personality includes a range of disorders such as infantile personalities, narcissistic personalities, antisocial personalities, as-if personalities, and schizoid personalities. In fact, any patient manifesting significant disturbance of identity in Kernberg's system is either psychotic or, if in possession of intact reality-testing, borderline.

In their emphasis on instincts, the theories of both Klein and Kernberg are more uncompromising than those of Freud. The main impact on psychoanalysis has been its stress on infants' ambivalent relationship with their mothers and the consequences of inadequate resolution. It should be noted, however, that Klein attaches little importance to the infant's actual experience of mothering. Thus, as her statements about the inner world of children are not linked to anything in the external world, her views are more or less impossible to verify empirically. Her numerous unwarranted assumptions concerning infants' fantasy lives must make us regard her theory with a certain scepticism. It is perhaps more important to stress the theoretical developments that Klein's ideas have stimulated than the ideas per se.

Fairbairn and Winnicott

Fairbairn (1952, 1963) and Winnicott (1953) were British psychoanalysts who were greatly affected by Melanie Klein's views on early development, although both found it hard to accept her emphasis on the classical theory of instincts (notably of innate aggression and destructiveness). Fairbairn considered the main source of motivation to be the establishment of a human relationship through which needs could safely be gratified. Thus Fairbairn reformulated Freud's theory of the libido. No longer was it seen as a system directing the person towards physical pleasure; rather, what impressed Fairbairn was its tendency to send individuals in search of particular patterns of relationships, in search of objects.

The essence of Fairbairn's approach lay in his emphasis on the strivings of the ego in its endeavour to reach an object (a person-relationship) from whom it might find support. For Fairbairn, the ego was not a mechanism of control over other psychic systems but was conceptualized as the self. He believed that the self was made up of internal images of past persons of importance to the individual. These internalized early relationships and the feelings that accompanied them, so he claimed, made up our current experience of ourselves.

One of Fairbairn's major contributions was the description of the schizoid personality. Such a person is not psychotic and may appear outwardly quite successful, but is in fact a solitary figure who, even when in a relationship, gives little or nothing to the other person. Fairbairn viewed this personality type as arising from a weak, underdeveloped self produced by the mother's failure to love the child for his/her own sake, to give the child spontaneous and genuine expressions of affection which the child could internalize and use as the basis of a sound ego-structure. This left the child unsure of the reality of his/her own ego (self) and therefore constantly playing a role, indulging in exhibitionism, and afraid that "giving" in a relationship might result in permanent loss or self-emptying.

Winnicott (1953) was also concerned with the earliest phase of the mother–child relationship and the importance of what he described as "good-enough" mothering for the child's personality development. The child's potential for development from absolute dependence to relative independence was, he believed, strongly influenced by the quality of maternal care. The earliest stage in the infant's experience is one of undifferentiated fusion with and attachment to his/her primary object, most likely the mother. The "good-enough" mother reflects this, and at the child's birth loves the baby as an extension of herself, thus enabling her to become emphatically tuned to the child's inner needs. As the child develops and becomes aware of his/her own needs and of the separate existence of the mother, the optimal mother–child relationship changes to allow a careful balance between gratification and frustration. The separation from the mother permits the infant to express his/her needs and initiative (the basis of the emerging sense of self). A mother who intrudes too much would short-circuit the infant's initiatives and restrict the development of the self. A too distant mother creates anxiety accompanied by the fading of the infant's internal representation of her. Either of these failures at "good-enough" mothering could result in the development of a "false self" based on the necessity for compliance with the demands of the external environment. As adults, such individuals would relate to the world through a compliant shell: they would not be entirely real to themselves or to others.

The transition from absolute dependence (undifferentiated fusion with mother) to relative dependence (awareness of mother's separateness) is accomplished, according to Winnicott, by the development of "transitional phenomena" of which the most obvious are transitional objects. These are often actual objects, such as a blanket, pillow, or favourite teddy bear, to which the child becomes intensely attached and separation from which stirs up extreme anxiety. Attachment to the object as an immediate displacement from attachment to the mother, enables the child gradually to separate from her. Children know that the blanket or teddy bear is not mother, and yet they react emotionally to these objects as if they were her. Such external objects, which offer comfort and security at times of anxiety and danger, permit children to explore the world around them more freely (Eagle, 1983).

Object-relations theory as outlined by Fairbairn, Winnicott, and other British psychoanalysts is currently perhaps the most widely accepted psychoanalytic approach in the United Kingdom. Its fundamental postulate, concerning the formative relationship between mother and infant during the first year of life, has become generally accepted in the psychoanalytic world.

However, whereas ego psychology attempted to improve psychoanalysis by refining its conceptual framework, object-relations theory introduced new concepts which, though not in direct conflict with empirical evidence, are none the less open to criticism. Many assumptions are made concerning the inner world of the infant which are difficult, if not impossible, to substantiate and are justified only if no simpler model can be advanced to account for the same data. Sandler and Sandler (1978) suggested that much of Fairbairn's and Winnicott's clinical material could be explained by a far less complex model. They put forward the idea that the fulfilment of wishes (seen by Freud as the gratification of instincts) could indeed be looked at in simpler terms, namely as the wish to repeat interactions that in the past had given pleasure or comfort. They proposed the theory that each partner in every relationship at any given time had a role for the other and explicitly (in real relationships) or implicitly (in fantasy) negotiated with that person in order to get them to respond in such a way as to restore the wished-for feeling of well-being and safety; for example, a young man might develop a relationship with a shy and diffident girl in order to restore the comfort he experienced in the early feeling of being totally in control of his mother. Many psychological problems could be looked at as being attempts to repeat comforting or gratifying early relationships. Thus an agoraphobic woman, whose fear so restricted her life that she stayed in bed most of the day, might actually be fulfilling a wish to have her husband "mother" her.

Kohut's theory

Kohut (1971), following similar lines to Winnicott, saw infants as perceiving the mother (the object) as part of themselves. Through her soothing and mirroring of infants' needs, she supplies them with the necessary functions of self-cohesion which infants cannot yet perform for themselves. Kohut suggested that when the child's self-love (narcissism) is undermined by the mother's inevitable occasional failure to provide care, the child defensively develops a protective, somewhat megalomaniac self-image (which Kohut termed the 'grandiose self'). The grandiose self is expected to moderate during maturation and in response to changes in the parents' responses: for example, a 2 year old who is able to ride a tricycle would receive attention and praise in contrast to an older sibling. It was suggested that narcissistic personality patterns are the result of the arrest of this normal developmental sequence. This childish grandiosity might remain unaltered if, for example, the mother's confirming responses were never forthcoming or where, alternatively, they were unpredictable or entirely unrealistic.

For Kohut and his North American followers the excessively unempathic responses of the self-objects result in the frustration of normal developmental needs and fixate the child's self at a fragile, archaic level. The narcissistic individual thus finds it necessary to make use of highly primitive self-object relationships (grandiosity, rage or excitement, or sedation through drugs or other addictions) to support self-cohesion as well as self-esteem. Such extremely sensitive individuals are said to be suffering from "narcissistic personality disorder". Kohut also evocatively described the subjective experience of emptiness that is secondary to an inadequately developed self. Such individuals tend to exploit others in social relationships and to treat their love objects as nothing more than extensions of themselves (Akhtar, Thomson, & Anderson, 1982). Lasch (1978) suggests that this personality type may be characteristic of contemporary western civilization.

This theory is essentially a deficiency theory: deficiency of necessary facilitating experiences leading to a psychic deficit (that is, an inadequately developed sense of self). The characteristic manifestations of the borderline states may be understood as indications of the individual's tragic attempts to cope with the profound limitations of his/her intra-psychic world. The clear therapeutic implication is that meaningful intervention must focus on the nature of the individual's deficit and, through a therapeutic environment that may be expected to lead to personal growth, make good the early deprivation: in Kohutian terms to provide a soothing and mirroring function leading to the restoration of the self.

PSYCHOANALYSIS

Although psychoanalytic theory has changed substantially since Freud's time, the treatment he pioneered remains relatively unchanged. The client (analysand) lies on a couch with the analyst sitting behind, out of the client's field of vision. The client is asked to talk honestly about whatever comes to mind and to follow the thoughts through, however embarrassing or trivial they might seem. In the United Kingdom, full psychoanalysis requires attendance for fifty-minute sessions five days per week over several years, although in some countries three or four sessions per week are regarded as sufficient.

The aim of psychoanalysis is the undoing of repression and other defences, the recovery of lost memories, and the achievement of insight or a fresh understanding of previously puzzling behaviour. The analysis may also provide a corrective emotional experience, in that the relationship with the analyst may help to undo the effects of previous deprivation (Alexander & French, 1946). As the analysis proceeds, the analytic situation encourages the development in the analysand of strong feelings for the analyst. The analyst gives little away about him- or herself, so that the influence of significant aspects of the clients' early relationships may be seen in their thoughts and fantasies about the analyst. This process, in which emotions rightly belonging to childhood relationships are transferred on to the analyst, is called *transference*.

The analyst's task is to clarify clients' emotional conflicts. This should start with the interpretation of their defences (for example the tendency to deal with anger by turning it on oneself). This can then be linked with past events to provide an account of the clients' forbidden impulses (for example anger aimed at an apparently uncaring mother). In doing this, the analyst works in the transference, allowing the analysand to feel these conflicts; thus anger towards the analyst for lateness or insufficient attentiveness may well feel frightening and be fended off initially, just as anger with mother was strongly defended against during childhood. In this way clients can work in the "here-and-now" with thoughts and feelings that belong in some way to the past. With a successful analysis, clients gain a better understanding of their behaviour in current relationships, in early relationships, and in the relationship with the analyst.

Thus psychoanalysis is aimed not at removing particular problem behaviours or symptoms but at a far-reaching and radical restructuring of the personality. How far it is successful in achieving this goal is a point of considerable contention. From a review of all studies of the effectiveness of psychoanalysis up to about 1990, Bachrach, Galatzer-Levy, Skolnikoff, and Waldron (1991) have shown that the rate of improvement, with symptom removal as the criterion, is about 64.5 per cent, which is roughly comparable to the effectiveness of other therapeutic approaches. There is little evidence concerning claims of more fundamental personality changes following full psychoanalysis. Such changes are in any case very difficult, if not impossible, to assess reliably. A tentative indication that full, five-times-weekly classical psychoanalysis may give the client something that alternative therapies do not, comes from studies of the client population of psychoanalysts. From a number of investigations it appears that more than half the patients of most psychoanalysts, at least in the United States, are mental health professionals, themselves involved in the administration of forms of therapy that have been advanced as alternatives to psychoanalysis (Kadushin, 1969).

PSYCHOANALYTIC PSYCHOTHERAPY

Psychoanalytic psychotherapy is practised much more widely than psychoanalysis, from which it has evolved. The analyst and client both sit in armchairs in full view of one another and meet only once or twice a week. The therapy tends to focus on specific psychological problems, to emphasize interpersonal events in the client's current life, and to consider the possible displacement of emotions from earlier relationships to current ones (generally excluding that with the analyst). Malan (1976), on the basis of some empirical evidence, strongly advocates the use of interpretations that emphasize the similarity between clients' responses to the analyst and to their parents. Some therapists go so far as to induce anxiety deliberately in their clients by provocative transference interpretations − for example, "You want to murder me just like you wanted to murder your father!" (Sifneos, 1972).

Many of these approaches aim at substantially shorter treatments than psychoanalysis and focus on a single conflict (for example, an inability to be assertive with father and hence with other male authority figures). Therapist and patient often make a "contract" for a particular number of sessions rather than entering an open-ended arrangement.

Such dynamically oriented psychotherapies rely on a distillation of fundamental psychoanalytic concerns: defences, drives, and the transference. In a number of studies (e.g., Sloane, Staples, Cristol, Yorkston, & Whipple, 1975) where the effectiveness of therapies based on psychoanalytic insights were contrasted clinically with that of other therapeutic approaches for neurotic problems, little difference in effectiveness was found. These are important findings since, while classical psychoanalysis compares very unfavourably with more modern therapeutic approaches in terms of time and cost, psychoanalytic psychotherapy is very much less intensive and in most cases takes no longer than do alternative modes of intervention.

Although in principle the practice of psychoanalysis requires lengthy specialist training, including the psychoanalysis of the trainee analyst, many clinical psychologists, as well as psychiatrists and social workers, practise psychotherapy guided by psychoanalytic principles without receiving a full psychoanalytic training.

EVALUATION

Finally, it must be asked, what is the value of the psychoanalytic approach? For psychology, its value is synonymous with its scientific status. Efforts have been made to demonstrate the scientific validity of psychoanalysis by replicating in the laboratory clinical phenomena such as projection, repression, and dream symbolism. These attempts constitute a substantial body of evidence, some consistent with and some failing to support psychoanalytic contentions (see reviews by Fisher & Greenberg, 1977; Fonagy, 1981; Kline, 1981). Although of great interest in their own right, such investigations have no real relevance to psychoanalysis. Attempting to replicate such complex processes as projection, for example, is impossible when so many of the factors normally responsible for their occurrence in real life and in the consulting room are absent in the laboratory.

This does not mean, however, that experimental investigations have no relevance to psychoanalysis. Experimentalists can examine the psychological processes that may underlie phenomena described in the clinical situation without attempting to recreate these phenomena in the laboratory. I have argued (Fonagy, 1982) that experimental studies cannot ever hope to validate psychoanalytic ideas in the sense of demonstrating their existence to observers not participating in the psychoanalytic encounter. Nevertheless, it is quite possible for laboratory studies to demonstrate the existence of psychological processes that underlie the phenomena described by psychoanalysts.

Taking this approach, we can be a little more optimistic about the potential scientific status of psychoanalysis. The rapid expansion of psychological knowledge has already provided much evidence consistent with psychoanalytic assumptions. Both psychoanalysis and psychology will continue to develop and grow for a long while yet. Eventually, adequate common ground may emerge so that psychoanalysis may become acceptable as a branch of psychological science. Until such a time, however, psychologists are correct in treating the unique but clinically based psychological models of psychoanalysts with interested and perhaps sympathetic scepticism.

FURTHER READING

Etchegoyen, R. (1991). *The foundations of psychoanalytic technique*. London: Karnac.

Greenberg, J. R., & Mitchell, S. A. (1983). *Object relations in psychoanalytic theory*. Cambridge, MA: Harvard University Press.

Sandler, J., Dare, C., & Holder, A. (1973). *The patient and the analyst: The basis of the psychoanalytic process*. London: Allen & Unwin.

Tyson, P., & Tyson, R. L. (1990). Psychoanalytic theories of development. New Haven, CT: Yale University Press.

REFERENCES

Akhtar, S., Thomson, J., & Anderson, T. (1982). Overview: Narcissistic personality disorder. *American Journal of Psychiatary*, *139*, 12–19.

Alexander, F., & French, T. M. (1946). *Psychoanalytic therapy*. New York: Ronald.

Bachrach, H. M., Galatzer-Levy, R., Skolnikoff, A., & Waldron, S., Jr (1991). On the efficacy of psychoanalysis. *Journal of the American Psychoanalytic Association*, *39*, 871–916.

Bion, W. R. (1957). Differentiation of the psychotic from the non-psychotic personalities. *International Journal of Psycho-Analysis*, *38*, 266–275.

Bion, W. R. (1962). Learning from experience. In W. R. Bion, *Seven servants: Four works by Wilfred R. Bion* (pp. 1–111). New York: Aronson, 1977.

Breuer, J., & Freud, S. (1895). *Studies on hysteria*. In J. Strachey (Ed. and trans.) *Standard edition of the complete psychological works of Sigmund Freud* (vol. 2). London: Hogarth.

Eagle, M. (1983). Interests as object relations. In J. Masling (Ed.) *Empirical studies of psychoanalytic theory* (pp. 159–187). Hillsdale, NJ: Analytic Press.

Erickson, E. H. (1959). Identity and the life cycle: Selected papers. *Psychological Issues*, Monograph vol. 1, whole no 41.

Fairbairn, R. (1952). *Object relations theory of the personality*. New York: Basic Books.

Fairbairn, R. (1963). Synopsis of an object-relations theory of the personality. *International Journal of Psychoanalysis*, *44*, 224–225.

Fisher, S., & Greenberg, R. (1977). *The scientific credibility of Freud's theories and therapy*. Brighton: Harvester.

Fonagy, P. (1981). Research on psychoanalytic concepts. In F. Fransella (Ed.) *Personality: Theory, measurement and research* (pp. 56–72). London: Methuen.

Fonagy, P. (1982). The integration of psychoanalysis and experimental science: A review. *International Review of Psychoanalysis, 9*, 125–145.

Freud, S. (1900). *The interpretation of dreams*. In J. Strachey (Ed. and trans.) *Standard edition of the complete psychological works of Sigmund Freud* (vols 4–5). London: Hogarth.

Freud, S. (1905). *Three essays on sexuality*. In J. Strachey (Ed. and trans.) *Standard edition of the complete psychological works of Sigmund Freud* (vol. 7). London: Hogarth.

Freud, S. (1923). *The ego and the id*. In J. Strachey (Ed. and trans.) *Standard edition of the complete psychological works of Sigmund Freud* (vol. 19). London: Hogarth.

Hartmann, H. (1958). *Ego psychology and the problem of adaptation*. New York: International Universities Press (original work published 1939).

Holt, R. R. (1976). Drive or wish: A reconsideration of the psychoanalytic theory of motivation. *Psychological Issues*, Monograph 36, 158–197.

Kadushin, C. (1969). *Why people go to psychiatrists*. New York: Atherton.

Kernberg, O. (1967). Borderline personality organization. *Journal of the American Psychoanalytic Association, 15*, 641–685.

Kernberg, O. (1975). *Borderline conditions and pathological narcissism*. New York: Aronson.

Kernberg, O. (1976). Technical considerations in the treatment of borderline personality organization. *Journal of the American Psychoanalytic Association, 24*, 795–829.

Kernberg, O. (1984). *Severe personality disorders: Psychotherapeutic strategies*. New Haven, CT: Yale University Press.

Klein, G. S. (1976). Freud's two theories of sexuality. *Psychological Issues*, Monograph 36, 14–70.

Klein, M. (1932). *The psycho-analysis of children*. London: Hogarth.

Klein, M. (1948). *Contributions to psycho-analysis. 1921–1945*. London: Hogarth.

Klein, M. (1957). Envy and gratitude. In M. Klein, *The writings of Melanie Klein* (vol. 3, pp. 176–235). London: Hogarth.

Kline, P. (1981). *Fact and fantasy in Freudian theory* (2nd edn). London: Methuen.

Kohut, H. (1971). *The analysis of the self*. New York: International Universities Press.

Lasch, C. (1978). *The culture of narcissism: American life in an age of diminishing expectations*. New York: Norton.

Malan, D. (1976). *Toward the validation of dynamic psychotherapy*. New York: Plenum.

O'Shaughnessy, E. (1981). A clinical study of a defensive organization. *International Journal of Psycho-Analysis, 62*, 359–369.

Rapaport, D. (1967). *The collected papers of David Rapaport*. New York: Basic Books.

Rosenfeld, H. (1987). *Impasse and interpretation*. London: Tavistock.

Sandler, J., & Sandler, A.-M. (1978). On the development of object relationships and affects. *International Journal of Psycho-Analysis, 59*, 285–296.

Segal, H. (1964). *Introduction to the work of Melanie Klein*. New York: Basic Books.

Sifneos, P. E. (1972). *Short-term psychotherapy and emotional crisis*. Cambridge, MA: Harvard University Press.

Sloane, R. B., Staples, F. R., Cristol, A. H., Yorkston, N. J., & Whipple, K. (1975). Short-term analytically oriented psychotherapy versus behavioral therapy. *American Journal of Psychiatry*, *132*, 373–377.

Sohn, L. (1985). Narcissistic organization, projective identification and the formation of the identificate. *International Journal of Psycho-Analysis*, *66*, 201–213.

Spillius, E. B. (1988). General introduction. In E. B. Spillius (Ed.) *Melanie Klein today: Developments in theory and practice* (vol. 1, pp. 1–7). London: Routledge.

Steiner, J. (1987). The interplay between pathological organizations and the paranoid-schizoid and depressive positions. *International Journal of Psycho-Analysis*, *68*, 69–80.

Winnicott, D. W. (1953). Transitional objects and transitional phenomena. *International Journal of Psychoanalysis*, *34*, 1–9.

GLOSSARY

This glossary is confined to a selection of frequently used terms that merit explanation or comment. Its informal definitions are intended as practical guides to meanings and usages. The entries are arranged alphabetically, word by word, and numerals are positioned as though they were spelled out.

abnormal psychology a branch of psychology, sometimes called psychopathology, concerned with the classification, aetiology (causation), diagnosis, treatment, and prevention of mental disorders and disabilities. *Cf.* clinical psychology.

acetylcholine one of the neurotransmitter (q.v.) substances that play a part in relaying information between neurons.

adrenal glands from the Latin *ad*, to, *renes*, kidneys, a pair of endocrine glands, situated just above the kidneys, which secrete adrenalin (epinephrine), noradrenalin (norepinephrine) (qq.v), and other hormones into the bloodstream. *See also* adrenocorticotropic hormone (ACTH).

adrenalin(e) hormone secreted by the adrenal glands (q.v.), causing an increase in blood pressure, release of sugar by the liver, and several other physiological reactions to perceived threat or danger. *See also* noradrenalin(e).

adrenocorticotropic hormone (ACTH) a hormone secreted by the pituitary gland that stimulates the adrenal gland to secrete corticosteroid hormones such as cortisol (hydrocortisone) into the bloodstream, especially in response to stress or injury.

agoraphobia from the Greek *agora*, market-place, *phobia*, fear, an irrational and debilitating fear of open places and of travelling or leaving home unaccompanied, often associated with panic attacks; one of the most common phobias (q.v.) encountered in clinical practice.

anal stage in psychoanalysis (q.v.), the second stage of psychosexual development, in approximately the second and third years of life, following the oral stage and preceding the phallic stage, characterized by preoccupation with the anus and derivation of pleasure from anal stimulation and defecation. *Cf.* genital stage, latency period, oral stage, phallic stage.

analytic psychology a school of psychoanalysis founded by the Swiss psychiatrist Carl Gustav Jung following a rift with Sigmund Freud.

anxiety disorders a group of mental disorders (q.v.) in which anxiety is an important symptom. *See also* obsessive-compulsive disorder, panic disorder, phobia, posttraumatic stress disorder (PTSD).

applied behaviour analysis the application of learning theory to behavioural problems in everyday settings, including hospitals, clinics, schools, and factories. Research and practice in this field is described by its practitioners as applied, behavioural, analytic, technological, conceptually systematic, effective, and capable of generalized effects. *See also* behaviour modification.

applied psychology the application of psychological theories and research findings to practical problems of everyday life. The major fields of applied psychology are the professions of clinical psychology, counselling psychology, educational (school) psychology, industrial (occupational) psychology, organizational psychology, and forensic (criminological) psychology (qq.v.).

archetypes according to the Swiss psychiatrist Carl Gustav Jung and his followers, universal, symbolic images that appear in myths, art, dreams, and other expressions of the collective unconscious.

autonomic nervous system a subdivision of the nervous system (q.v.) that regulates (autonomously) the internal organs and glands. It is divided into the sympathetic nervous system and the parasympathetic nervous system (qq.v.).

behaviour modification the application of techniques of operant conditioning (q.v.) to reduce or eliminate maladaptive or problematic behaviour patterns or to develop new ones. *See also* applied behaviour analysis, cognitive-behaviour therapy, flooding.

behaviour therapy a therapeutic technique based on the principles of conditioning and behaviour modification (qq.v.).

behavioural medicine an interdisciplinary field of study devoted to behavioural aspects of health and illness.

bipolar disorder a mood disorder (q.v.) in which depression alternates with mania (q.v.), also known as manic-depressive psychosis.

borderline personality disorder a mental disorder in which a person hovers on the borderline between normal and disordered functioning, typically with disturbed social relations, dramatic mood swings, and often outbursts of anger and impulsive episodes of antisocial behaviour.

case-study a research method involving a detailed investigation of a single individual or a single organized group, used extensively in clinical psychology and less often in other branches of psychology.

catecholamine any member of the group of hormones (q.v.) that are catechol derivatives, especially adrenalin, noradrenalin, and dopamine, (qq.v.), all of which are involved in the functioning of the nervous system (q.v.).

central nervous system (CNS) in human beings and other vertebrates, the brain and spinal cord.

client-centred therapy a method of psychotherapy (q.v.) or counselling pioneered by the American psychologist Carl Rogers in which the therapist refrains from advising, suggesting, or persuading, but tries instead to establish empathy with the client by clarifying and reflecting back the client's expressed feelings; the therapist tries to convey an attitude of "unconditional positive regard" in the context of a permissive, non-threatening relationship, hence this method of psychotherapy is also called non-directive therapy or non-directive counselling.

clinical psychology one of the major professions of psychology, concerned with the prevention, diagnosis, treatment, and study of mental disorders and disabilities, to be distinguished from abnormal psychology (q.v.), which is the academic study of these matters.

CNS *see* central nervous system (CNS).

cognition from the Latin *cognoscere*, to know, attention, thinking, problem-solving, remembering, and all other mental processes that fall under the general heading of information processing.

cognitive-behaviour therapy techniques of psychotherapy based on methods of behaviour modification (q.v.) with an emphasis on the learning of cognitive responses involving imagery, fantasy, thoughts, and above all beliefs.

compulsions repetitive, ritualised, stereotyped actions, such as hand-washing, that a person feels unable to stop performing in spite of realizing that the behaviour is inappropriate or excessive, often associated with obsessions (q.v.).

continuous reinforcement in learning theory, a schedule of reinforcement (q.v.) in which every response is reinforced. *Cf.* intermittent (partial) reinforcement.

counselling psychology a branch of applied psychology, related to clinical psychology (q.v.), devoted to helping people to solve problems of everyday living through advice-giving.

counter-transference in psychoanalysis, the displacement by an analyst on to a client of emotions, often sexually charged, from earlier relationships. *Cf.* transference.

criminological psychology *see* forensic (criminological) psychology.

defence mechanisms a term used originally in psychoanalysis (q.v.) and later more widely in psychology and psychiatry to refer to patterns of feeling, thought, or behaviour that arise in response to perceptions of psychic danger and enable a person to avoid conscious awareness of conflicts or anxiety-arousing stressors; among the most important are denial, displacement, intellectualization, projection, rationalization, reaction formation, regression, and repression (qq.v.).

delusion a false personal belief, maintained in the face of overwhelming contradictory evidence, excluding religious beliefs that are widely accepted by members of the person's culture or sub-culture, characteristic especially of delusional (paranoid) disorder (q.v.). *Cf.* hullucination.

delusional (paranoid) disorder formerly called paranoia, a mental disorder characterized by delusions (q.v.), especially of jealousy, grandeur, or persecution, but with otherwise unimpaired intellectual functioning.

denial a defence mechanism (q.v.) involving a failure to acknowledge some aspect of reality that would be apparent to other people.

depression a sustained negative mood state characterized by sadness, pessimism, a general feeling of despondency, passivity, indecisiveness, suicidal thoughts, sleep disturbances, and other mental and physical symptoms, associated with some mood disorders (q.v.).

desensitization, systematic a technique of behaviour therapy or behaviour modification (qq.v.) used for eliminating phobias (q.v.) in which the individual is exposed to a graded hierarchy of anxiety-eliciting stimuli under conditions of deep relaxation until the most frightening item can be confronted without tension.

displacement a defence mechanism (q.v.) involving redirection of feelings about a person or object on to another, usually less threatening target.

dopamine a catecholamine (q.v.); one of the neurotransmitter (q.v.) substances significantly involved in central nervous system (q.v.) functioning.

DSM-IV the common name of the fourth edition of the *Diagnostic and Statistical Manual of Mental Disorders* of the American Psychiatric Association, published in 1994, replacing DSM-III-R, the revised version of the third edition published in 1987, containing the most authoritative classification and definitions of mental disorders (q.v.).

ECT *see* electroconvulsive therapy (ECT).

educational (school) psychology one of the major professions of psychology, devoted to psychological factors affecting learning, adjustment, and behaviour in children, and the application of psychological methods to provide practical help to children with learning or behaviour problems and to their teachers and parents.

ego from the Latin word for I, in English language versions of psychoanalysis one of the three major divisions of the psyche, and the one that is conscious and governed by the reality principle (q.v.); Freud originally used the more familiar and informal German word *Ich*, which also means I. *Cf.* id, superego.

ego ideal *see under* superego.

electroconvulsive therapy (ECT) a psychiatric method of treating certain symptoms of mental disorder by passing a weak electric current (20–30 milliamps) through the brain to induce *grand mal* epileptic-type convulsions in patients who are usually first given sedative and muscle relaxant drugs. Sometimes called shock therapy or electroshock therapy (EST).

emotion from the Latin *e*, away, *movere*, to move, any evaluative, affective, intentional, short-term psychological state.

engineering psychology *see* ergonomics.

ergonomics from the Greek *ergon*, work, *nomia*, law, a branch of industrial (occupational) and organizational psychology (q.v.) concerned with designing jobs, equipment, and workplaces to maximize performance and well-being and to minimize accidents, fatigue, boredom, and energy expenditure, also called engineering psychology, especially in the United States.

5-hydroxytryptamine (5-HT) another name for serotonin (q.v.).

flooding a technique of behaviour therapy (q.v.) for treating phobias (q.v.) in which the client is exposed to the phobic stimulus for extended periods of time without the opportunity of escape.

forensic (criminological) psychology a branch of applied psychology concerned with all aspects of criminal behaviour and the application of psychology to practical problems of crime and punishment.

free association a therapeutic technique, used in psychoanalysis (q.v.) for recovering unconscious material, in which clients are encouraged to verbalize their stream of consciousness without hesitation or censorship.

genital stage in psychoanalysis (q.v.), the final stage of psychosexual development, beginning in early adolescence following the latency period (q.v.), characterized by affectionate sexual relationships with members of the opposite sex. *Cf.* anal stage, latency period, oral stage, phallic stage.

Gestalt therapy a method of psychotherapy devised by Fritz Perls in the United States in the 1960s in which clients are encouraged to concentrate on the immediate present and to express their true feelings openly.

hallucination from the Latin *alucinari*, to wander in the mind, a false perception, most commonly visual or auditory, subjectively similar or identical to an ordinary perception but occurring in the absence of relevant sensory stimuli, characteristic in particular of some forms of schizophrenia. False perceptions occurring during sleep, while falling asleep (hypnagogic image), or while awakening (hypnopompic image) are not normally considered to be hallucinations. *Cf.* delusion.

hormone from the Greek *horman*, to stir up or urge on, a chemical substance secreted into the bloodstream by an endocrine gland and transported to another part of the body where it exerts a specific effect.

id from the Latin word meaning it, in English language versions of psychoanalysis (q.v.) one of the three major divisions of the psyche, governed by the pleasure principle (q.v.), from which come blind, instinctual impulses towards the immediate gratification of primitive urges. Freud originally used the more informal and familiar German word *Es*, which also means it. *Cf.* ego, superego.

industrial (occupational) and organizational psychology one of the major fields of applied psychology (q.v.), sometimes called work psychology, concerned with the application of psychological knowledge to problems of people in work and unemployment and with the structures and functions of organizations and the activities of people within them. *See also* ergonomics.

intellectualization a defence mechanism (q.v.) involving excessive abstract thinking designed to block out disturbing emotions.

intermittent (partial) reinforcement in learning theory, any schedule of reinforcement (q.v.) in which not all responses are reinforced. *Cf.* continuous reinforcement.

latency period in psychoanalysis (q.v.), the period following the phallic stage but preceding the genital stage, from about the age of 5 until early adolescence, during which the sexual drive is thought to be sublimated. *Cf.* anal stage, genital stage, oral stage, phallic stage.

learning the relatively permanent change in behaviour that occurs as a result of experience. *See also* operant conditioning.

libido from the Latin word for desire, in psychoanalysis (q.v.), psychic energy emanating from the id (q.v.).

locus of control in personality theory and social psychology, the perceived source of control over one's behaviour, on a scale from internal to external.

mania a mood disorder characterized by extreme elation, expansiveness, irritability, talkativeness, inflated self-esteem, and flight of ideas.

manic-depressive psychosis *see* bipolar disorder.

mental disorder according to DSM-IV (q.v.), a psychological or behavioural syndrome or pattern associated with distress (a painful symptom), disability (impairment in one or more areas of functioning), and a significantly increased risk of death, pain, disability, or an important loss of freedom, occurring not merely as a predictable response to a disturbing life-event.

mood disorders a group of mental disorders characterized by disturbances of affect or mood, including especially depression, bipolar disorder and mania (qq.v.).

motivation the driving forces responsible for the initiation, persistence, direction, and vigour of goal-directed behaviour.

multiple personality disorder a rare dissociative disorder in which two or more markedly different personalities coexist within the same individual, popularly confused with schizophrenia (q.v.).

negative reinforcement reinforcement (q.v.) that results from the removal rather than the presentation of the reinforcer (which, by implication, is an aversive or punishing negative reinforcer). *Cf.* positive reinforcement.

nervous system *see under* autonomic nervous system, central nervous system (CNS), parasympathetic nervous system, sympathetic nervous system.

neuron from the Greek word for nerve, a nerve cell, which is the basic structural and functional unit of the nervous system, consisting of a cell body, axon, and dendrites.

neurophysiology the study of the operation of the nervous system (q.v.).

neurosis an obsolescent umbrella term for a group of mental disorders that are distressing but do not involve gross impairment of psychological functioning or any loss of self-insight or contact with reality. *See* anxiety disorders, obsessive-compulsive disorder, panic disorder, phobia, post-traumatic stress disorder (PTSD).

neurotransmitter a chemical substance such as acetylcholine, dopamine, serotonin, or noradrenalin (qq.v.) by which a neuron (q.v.) communicates with another neuron or with a muscle or gland.

nondirective therapy (counselling) *see* client-centred therapy.

noradrenalin one of the catecholamine (q.v.) hormones and an important neurotransmitter (q.v.) in the nervous system, also called norepinephrine, especially in United States usage.

norepinephrine *see* noradrenalin.

observational learning *see* vicarious learning.

obsessions recurrent, persistent, irrational ideas, thoughts, images, or impulses that are experienced not as voluntary but as unwanted invasions of consciousness, characteristic especially of obsessive-compulsive disorder (q.v.).

obsessive-compulsive disorder one of the more common anxiety disorders characterized, as the name suggests, by obsessions and compulsions (qq.v).

occupational psychology a British term for the branch of applied psychology concerned with all aspects of psychology in the workplace and is commonly referred to in the United States as industrial/organizational (I/O) psychology.

Oedipus complex in psychoanalysis (q.v.), a normally unconscious desire in a child, especially a boy, to possess sexually the parent of the opposite sex and to exclude the parent of the same sex. It is named after a character in Greek mythology who killed his father, being unaware of his kinship, and unwittingly married his mother.

operant conditioning a type of learning, sometimes called instrumental conditioning, which focuses on the process by which behaviour changes as a result of its consequences, in particular the way in which an individual's behavioural responses become more or less frequent as a consequence of reinforcement (q.v.).

oral stage in psychoanalysis (q.v.), the earliest, infantile, stage of psychosexual development during which the libido (q.v.) focuses on the mouth and has not been differentiated, so the ingestion of food has a sexual quality and pleasure is derived from sucking, chewing, licking, and biting. *Cf.* anal stage, genital stage, latency period, phallic stage.

organizational psychology *see under* industrial (occupational) and organizational psychology.

panic disorder an anxiety disorder characterized by panic attacks, overwhelming apprehension, dread or terror, fear of going insane or dying, and fight or flight behaviour.

paranoia *see* delusional (paranoid) disorder.

parapraxis (pl. parapraxes), in psychoanalysis (q.v.) an everyday absent-minded error, such as a slip of the tongue, assumed to be caused by repressed impulses.

parasympathetic nervous system one of the two major divisions of the autonomic nervous system (q.v.); its general function is to conserve metabolic energy. *Cf.* sympathetic nervous system.

partial reinforcement *see* intermittent (partial) reinforcement.

personality from the Latin *persona*, mask, the sum total of all the behavioural and mental characteristics that distinguish an individual from others.

personality disorder any of a group of mental disorders (q.v.) characterized by deeply ingrained, enduring, maladaptive patterns of behaviour that cause suffering to the person with the disorder or to others.

phallic stage in psychoanalysis (q.v.), a stage of psychosexual development following the anal stage but before the latency period, between the ages of about 2 and 5, characterized by preoccupation with the penis or clitoris. *Cf.* anal stage, genital stage, latency period, oral stage.

phobia from the Greek *phobos*, fear, an irrational, debilitating, persistent, and intense fear of a specific type of object, activity, or situation, which, if certain diagnostic criteria are fulfilled, may be considered a mental disorder (q.v.). *See also* agoraphobia.

physiological psychology the branch of psychology concerned with the relationships between physiological and psychological processes.

pleasure principle in psychoanalysis (q.v.), the doctrine that psychological processes and behaviour are governed by the gratification of needs. It is seen as the governing process of the id (q.v.), in contrast to the reality principle (q.v.) which is the governing process of the ego (q.v.).

positive reinforcement a process of reinforcement (q.v.) in which the relative frequency of the response is increased by the presentation of a reinforcer with rewarding properties. *Cf.* negative reinforcement.

post-traumatic stress disorder (PTSD) an anxiety disorder resulting from experience of a major traumatic event, characterized by obsessive reliving of the trauma in fantasies and dreams, a feeling of emotional numbness and lack of engagement in the world, sleep disturbances, an exaggerated startle response, general symptoms of anxiety, and in some cases (e.g. survivors of concentration camps) guilt about having survived.

projection a defence mechanism (q.v.) in which unacknowledged feelings, impulses, or thoughts are falsely attributed to other people.

projective tests psychological tests designed to tap deep-lying psychological processes, usually consisting of weakly structured or ambiguous stimulus materials on to which the perceiver is assumed to project ideas, which may be unconscious. *See also* Rorschach test, Thematic Apperception Test (TAT).

psychoanalysis a theory of mental structure and function and a method of psychotherapy based on the writings of Sigmund Freud and his followers, focusing primarily on unconscious mental processes and the various defence mechanisms that people use to repress them. *See also* anal stage, defence mechanisms, ego, free association, genital stage, id, latency period, libido, Oedipus complex, oral stage, phallic stage, pleasure principle, reality principle, sublimation, superego, transference, unconscious.

psychodynamic relating to psychological systems and theories that place heavy emphasis on motivation (q.v.), especially psychoanalysis (q.v.) and its offshoots.

psychometrics from the Greek *psyche*, mind, *metron*, measure, mental testing, including IQ, ability, and aptitude testing and the use of psychological tests for measuring interests, attitudes, and personality traits and for diagnosing mental disorders.

psychosis gross impairment of psychological functioning, including loss of self-insight and of contact with reality, such as is found in mental disorders involving hallucinations and delusions (qq.v.). *Cf.* neurosis.

psychotherapy the treatment of mental disorders by psychological methods. *See also* behaviour modification, behaviour therapy, client-centred therapy, cognitive-behaviour therapy, flooding, Gestalt therapy, psychoanalysis, rational-emotive therapy, systematic desensitization, token economy.

rational-emotive therapy a method of psychotherapy originated by the American psychologist Albert Ellis in which the therapist actively challenges the irrational beliefs of the client.

rationalization a defence mechanism (q.v.) in which false but reassuring or self-serving explanations are contrived to explain one's own or others' behaviour.

reaction formation a defence mechanism (q.v.) in which a person replaces unacceptable thoughts, feelings, or behaviour with ones that are diametrically opposite.

reality principle in psychoanalysis (q.v.), the governing principle of the ego (q.v.), which exerts control over behaviour to meet the demands and constraints imposed by the external world. *Cf.* pleasure principle.

regression a defence mechanism (q.v.) in which an adult: or an adolescent behaves in a manner more appropriate to a child in order to avoid or reduce anxiety.

reinforcement in learning theory, the strengthening of the bond between a stimulus and a response, or anything that increases the relative frequency of a response.

reinforcer any stimulus or event that increases the relative frequency of a response during the process of reinforcement (q.v.).

repression a defence mechanism (q.v.) involving an inability to recall disturbing desires, feelings, thoughts, or experiences.

Rorschach test a projective test (q.v.) named after the Swiss psychiatrist Hermann Rorschach consisting of 10 cards on which are printed bilaterally symmetrical inkblots to which the testee responds by describing what the inkblots look like or what they bring to mind.

schedules of reinforcement in operant conditioning (q.v.), a rule describing the functional relationship between reinforcement (q.v.) and an organism's responses. In a fixed ratio (FR) schedule, reinforcement occurs regularly after a fixed number of responses; in a fixed interval (FI) schedule, reinforcement occurs after fixed intervals irrespective of the organism's responses; variable ratio (VR) and variable interval (VI) schedules are defined *mutatis mutandis*.

schizophrenia from the Greek *schizein*, to split, *phren*, mind, a group of mental disorders characterized by incoherent thought and speech, hallucinations (q.v.), delusions (q.v.), flattened or inappropriate affect, deterioration of social functioning, and lack of self-care. In spite of its derivation, the word does not refer to multiple personality disorder (q.v.).

school psychology *see* educational (school) psychology.

serotonin one of the neurotransmitter (q.v.) substances in the nervous system, also known as 5-hydroxytryptamine or 5-HT.

shaping a method of training animals and people to exhibit novel forms of behaviour by using a suitable schedule of reinforcement to reward successive approximations to the target behaviour, beginning with existing elements of the subject's behavioural repertoire.

social learning learning that occurs through observation of the behaviour of others, called models, together with imitation, and vicarious learning (q.v.).

social skills a class of abilities to perform the forms of verbal and non-verbal behaviour required for competent social interaction in order to produce desired effects on other people.

stressor any stimulus, event or state of affairs that causes stress.

sublimation in psychoanalysis (q.v.), the redirection of libido or psychic energy originating in sexual impulses into non-sexual, especially artistic or creative activity.

superego in English language versions of psychoanalysis (q.v.), one of the three major divisions of the psyche, which develops out of a conflict between the id and the ego (qq.v.) and incorporates the moral standards of society. It consists of two parts: the ego ideal (a narcissistic image of one's own perfection and omnipotence) and the conscience (one's moral scruples, the part of the superego said to be most readily soluble in alcohol).

sympathetic nervous system one of the two major divisions of the autonomic nervous system (q.v.); it is concerned with general activation, and it mobilizes the body's reaction to stress or perceived danger. *Cf.* parasympathetic nervous system.

systematic desensitization a technique of behaviour therapy (q.v.) pioneered by the South African psychiatrist Joseph Wolpe for treating phobias and specific anxieties, in which the client enters a state of deep muscle relaxation and is then exposed to a hierarchy of progressively more anxiety-arousing situations, real or imagined.

Thematic Apperception Test (TAT) a projective test (q.v.) based on a series of somewhat ambiguous pictures about which the testee is asked to tell imaginative stories.

token economy a method of behaviour modification (q.v.) in which people living in an institution or other controllable environment are assigned target behaviour patterns and are rewarded for achieving them with tokens that they can exchange for privileges.

transference in psychoanalysis, the displacement by a client on to an analyst of emotions, often sexually charged, that have been carried over (transferred) from earlier relationships, especially with parents. *Cf.* counter-transference.

unconscious occurring without awareness or intention; in psychoanalysis (q.v.), the name for the part of the mind containing instincts, impulses, images, and ideas of which one is not normally aware.

vicarious learning from the Latin *vicarius*, substituted, learning that occurs through the observation of others' behaviour and its consequences, also called observational learning. *See also* social learning.

INDEX